Plays
by
Daniel Damiano
Volume 1

Harmony Park

*

The Golden Year

*

The Dishonorable Discharge of Private Pitts

Plays by Daniel Damiano, Volume 1
Copyright © 2022 by Daniel Damiano

ISBN: 979-8-218-06116-6 (Paperback)

Original Copyright:
The Golden Year © 2010 by Daniel Damiano
The Dishonorable Discharge of Private Pitts © 2013 by Daniel Damiano
Harmony Park © 2015 by Daniel Damiano

fandango 4 Art House

Publisher's Note: These are works of fiction. Names, characters, places, and incidents are a product of the author's imagination.

Production Photo Credits (Cover):
Harmony Park – Photographed by Detroit Repertory Theatre
(World Premiere – Detroit Repertory Theatre, MI, 2018 –
Pictured l-r, Harold Uriah Hogan, Samer Ajluni and Aaron Kottke.)
The Golden Year – Photographed by Jim Del Giudice
(World Premiere – WorkShop Theater, NYC, 2013 –
Pictured l-r, Ellen Barry and Gerry Goodstein.)
The Dishonorable Discharge of Private Pitts – Photographed by Gerry Goodstein
(World Premiere – fandango 4 Art House, NYC, 2015 –
Pictured l-r, Brooke Turner and Galen-Murphy Hoffman.)

"*The Golden Year* is 24 Karat! - Every once in a while, an off-off-Broadway production jumps up and reminds you that there is some really good Theatre happening up and down the side streets of Manhattan. *The Golden Year*, Daniel Damiano's 90-minute comedy-with-substance is one such example."
- Phil Dorian, Scene on Stage

"The plight of the retiree is one you rarely encounter in drama. But in a world where the aging, trusty systems are coming apart, there are just as many questions on the other side of 65 as there are on the way up, which *The Golden Year* eloquently raises."
- Jenna Scherer, Time Out NY

"*The Golden Year* Shines! - *The Golden Year* may have been at the Workshop Theatre off-Broadway, but this play has Broadway potential. - Damiano's insight into a newly retired couple's approach to life, their supportive relationship and the new predicaments they find themselves in is beautifully crafted."
- Ruth Antrich, Times Square Chronicles

"The WorkShop Theater has a long list of world premieres to its credit, none more worthy than Damiano's enjoyably insightful one-act play - ... destined for a wider audience..."
- Fred Winship, UPI International

"*The Golden Year* is poised for an open-ended run at a suitable New York theater, and is a natural for regional theater."
- Don Collester, WDVR Radio, NJ

Praise for
THE DISHONORABLE DISCHARGE
OF PRIVATE PITTS
(World Premiere with fandango 4 Art House, NYC, 2015)

"This play is a heroic underdog that points a dirty yet necessary mirror back at its viewers. I actually cried in a public setting (something

I typically refuse to do). - This play deserves a longer run and more attention – and while it has a quaint home now in the meager space in which it currently reigns, it's sad to think of how many plays out there are thriving on half of the valor and entertainment that *The Dishonorable Discharge of Private Pitts* beholds."
- Louis DeVaughn Nelson, Center On the Aisle

"*The Dishonorable Discharge of Private Pitts* moves us to reexamine our values of faith and our community in the face of war. It is an intimate character-shifting ensemble epic. - Presenting his harsh criticisms of the war in a cool-headed way, Damiano creates a paradigm of America as a nation struggling to makeover its crooked warmongering image. - *The Dishonorable Discharge of Private Pitts* leaves a lasting and pressing impression."
- Artem Yatsunov, Theatre is Easy

"Powerful, with captivating scenes that evince emotion and point to the institutional flaws we often blindly accept in the realms of parenting, in religion, and in the military. – *The Dishonorable Discharge of Private Pitts* is heartfelt."
- ReviewsHub

A WORD FROM A PLAYWRIGHT

The three plays assembled in this collection, while they differ somewhat stylistically, are united in being character-based works with a strong social relevance. In *Harmony Park*, it is the relations among a multi-ethnic landscaping crew in Queens, NY. In *The Golden Year*, it is the depiction of a Long Island couple and the unanticipated realities that ensue at the onset of their retirement. And, lastly, in *The Dishonorable Discharge of Private Pitts*, it is the journey of a young Texas woman whose life is given direction and is just as quickly led astray by her country's involvement in the Iraq War.

Please note that these are not acting editions and, as of this writing, are not published as such. Therefore, if you have interest in in any of these plays for production, please reach out to the publisher through www.fandango4arthouse.weebly.com or through the playwright's direct website at www.danieldamiano.com.

All that said, to anyone who has come upon these plays simply as a curious reader, I thank you for your curiosity.

And to the artist in any field who feels cast aside or that their talent and passion have been rendered insignificant by the absence of mass acknowledgement and adoration, please know that you are a success still – for all who seek to create and share their soulful creations with the world *are*.

- *Daniel Damiano, 6/9/22*

Plays

HARMONY PARK

HARMONY PARK

Harmony Park received its World Premiere with Detroit Repertory Theatre with the following cast and production staff, March/April 2018:

ERNIE……….……..Harold Uriah Hogan
MIKE………………...…Aaron Kottke
JOSE……………………….Samer Ajluni
SAM………………………..Mark Bishop

Directed by Barbara Busby

Stage Manager: Dan Jaroslaw
Lighting Designer: Thomas Schraeder
Sound Designer: Burr Huntington
Set Designer: Harry Wetzel
Lighting Technician: Cornell Markham
Literary Manager: Leah Smith
Artistic Director: Bruce E. Milan

Special Thanks to the following artists who lent their talents to previous readings of *Harmony Park*:

Philip Callen, Keldrick Crowder, David McElwee
and DeLance Minefee, directed by Justin Lord
(for Urban Stages, NYC), and Matt Antar, Leonard Dozier
and Joseph Franchini, directed by Paula D'Alessandris
(for fandango 4 Art House, NYC)

Cast of Characters

ERNIE - *Mid-to-late 50s. African-American, burly, from the Bronx. Wise, cultured, self-educated, self-made in many respects. Landscaping crew foreman.*

MIKE – *Mid-to-late 20s. White, lanky, Italian-American , from Brooklyn. Honest, talkative, curious, in sync with Ernie's sense of humor. Landscaper.*

JOSE – *Mid-to-late 40s. Puerto Rican, from Queens. Neurotic, good humored. Long-time assistant foreman to Ernie.*

SAM – *Mid 40s. White, stocky, Polish-American, from Brooklyn. Tough, sense of humor, at a more vulnerable stage.*

The play is set in an unnamed and somewhat precarious section of Queens, at the excavated site of a soon-to-be park, which develops over the course of the play.

Spring to Fall

2015

ACT ONE

Scene 1

ERNIE & MIKE, lunchtime, on site.

ERNIE: You hear the one about the fake pregnant lady?

MIKE: The what? Fake…?

ERNIE: *(Over "Fake…")* Fake pregnant lady, yeah. You heard about 'er?

MIKE: 'is a joke?

ERNIE: No, it ain't no joke, man. Met 'er myself on the Q27 bus.

MIKE: What, you date 'er?

ERNIE: Kiss my ass.

MIKE: How do you know she wasn't really pregnant?

ERNIE: Well, listen to this. Saw this woman once every week or so for like 5 months, right? Always at rush hour. Always a jammed bus. She gets on, lookin' ready to pop. Everybody sittin' hops up, so she always gotta' seat, right?

MIKE: Yeah.

ERNIE: So this was how it went every time I saw her. n'I'm always lookin' at 'er thinkin', man, I hope someone on this bus knows how to deliver 'cause, I mean, she was at the tippin' point, y'know?

MIKE: Okay.

ERNIE: But after a while, I see 'er and I'm thinkin', is it me or has this lady looked 10 months pregnant for the last 5 months.

MIKE: What?!

ERNIE: Well, sonofabitch, one day this woman gets on, jammed bus, rush hour, all that. Only now she looks the biggest I ever seen 'er. I mean like huge! Like she about t'give entry to a toddler with gigantism or some shit.

MIKE: What the fuck…?

ERNIE: No, wait now. So she's got her raincoat on with this huge, HUGE bulgin' belly.

MIKE: Oh, man…

ERNIE: Ain't even rainin' n'it's about an 80 degree day, t'boot, okay?

MIKE: Okay.

ERNIE: She does her lil' maneuverin' through the crowd. All the ones sittin' in her eyeshot jump right up like fuckin' Jack'n the boxes, and she goes t'sit, right?

MIKE: Yeah.

ERNIE: 'cept this time, as she's about t'sit, a motherfuckin' Butterball turkey drops right outa' her raincoat and hits the floor like a damn bowlin' ball.

MIKE: *(Laughs…)* Fuck…!

ERNIE: Wait, wait, wait…

MIKE: Holy shit…

ERNIE: Wait now… So she goes to get it, but she can't bend over because she's got another one in there…

MIKE: Another fuckin' turkey…?!

7

ERNIE: *(Over "turkey...")* Lady had two motherfuckin' 20 lb turkeys n'they both dropped outa' her like A-bombs!

MIKE: What the fuck???!!!

ERNIE: God as my witness.

MIKE: So the jig was up.

ERNIE: Yeah, t'everyone on the bus.

MIKE: What the hell she do?

ERNIE: She picked 'em up n' held 'em in her arms like newborns for like 10 blocks...

MIKE: Hah...!

ERNIE: Her stop comes, she gets up, someone yells out –
"Fake pregnant lady with two turkeys comin' through!!!"

MIKE: You are fuckin'...

ERNIE: No shit.

MIKE: Jesus...

ERNIE: Coupla' weeks go by, I don't see hide nor hair from her, right? Then one day I'm comin' to work on the train, open up the paper – there she is. Busted!

MIKE: Holy shit.

ERNIE: Over the course a' like 8 months, she lifted about 20 turkeys, hams n'pork loins from two different Key Foods n'a C-Town. All on surveillance.

MIKE: Tsch...

ERNIE: Even had a damn tarot card readin' scam goin' too.

MIKE: A fuckin' grifter.

ERNIE: n'God knows what else.

MIKE: For like 8 months she was gettin' away with this?

ERNIE: Yep.

MIKE: What kinda' surveillance?

ERNIE: Well, my thinkin' is that they didn't exactly have Pentagon-level security at these supermarkets, so they likely needed to be tipped off from someone on the outside.

MIKE: But I mean, it's not like she was goin' in lookin' pregnant.

ERNIE: I know.

MIKE: She goes in normal n'comes out with a bun in the oven n'no one batted an eye the whole time?

ERNIE: Seasoned con artists know how to blend in, I guess.

MIKE: Unbefuckinlievable…

ERNIE: Lived here all my life'n it never ceases to amaze me.

MIKE: Jesus…

    (A moment, as they eat…)

MIKE: You ever go to the San Genero festival?

ERNIE: What, the Little Italy thing with the zeppoles n'shit?

MIKE: Yeah.

ERNIE: Nah, never did.

MIKE: Well, this was before Little Italy was Huge Chinatown like it is now.

ERNIE: Yeah, alright.

MIKE: My mother used t'take us every summer. n'every summer there'd be this fake nun.

ERNIE: *(Snickers...)* Fake nun.

MIKE: Looked jus' like Mother Theresa too. Sandpaper Italian accent, the whole outfit, walkin' around with a fuckin' teak salad bowl'n this name tag, which I guess was supposed t'show that she was certified or somethin'. I dunno'. But anyway, she was a fuckin' flim-flammer. Didn't even know it either until years later.

ERNIE: Looka' that.

MIKE: n'all the vendors knew she was fake. She was like a mascot.

ERNIE: I believe it.

MIKE: You'd go'n get a sausage n'she would appear outa' the blue like an apparition with this fuckin' salad bowl.

ERNIE: Your mother never got hip to her?

MIKE: Fuck no. Are you kiddin'. Ol' school catholic like my mother? No, she gave t'her every fuckin' time. Every time we went to the festival, my mother musta' spent an extra $20 we didn't have on a cause that didn't even exist.

ERNIE: Hm.

MIKE: I brought it up to her a few years ago too.

ERNIE: The nun?

MIKE: Yeah, told 'er she was fake. Didn't wana' hear it.

ERNIE: Wow.

MIKE: Didn't wana' fuckin' hear it. Had a whole argument about it. She even threw a fuckin' brussel sprout at my head.

> *(ERNIE laughs…)*

Yeah, it's funny when she's not your mother.

ERNIE: She probably believed ya' n'was jus' embarrassed she fell for it.

MIKE: Ern, c'mon, with all I've told you about her?

ERNIE: Hey, jus' tryin' t'give her the benefit a' the doubt.

MIKE: Don't. My mother believes a lota' crazy shit, Ern. 'at's the least of it, believe me.

ERNIE: Alright, well…

MIKE: *(Takes a bite…)* F'Godsakes, she thought my father was gonna' come back after he took the car and cashed out their bank accounts. What does *'at* tell ya'?

ERNIE: You never told me he cashed out their savings.

MIKE: Everything, Ern.

ERNIE: Damn…

MIKE: n'yet she still made dinner for him every night for like 2 months.

ERNIE: Like she jus' had it in the oven for 'im?

MIKE: In the oven? She had it sittin' at the dining table with an open beer bottle.

ERNIE: No shit.

11

MIKE: Is 'at denial or what?

ERNIE: Yeah, that's swimmin' in it.

MIKE: We're at the table lookin' at this empty seat, like we're eatin' with the Invisible Man or some shit. She hadn't worked in years, had t'go back to work. My brothers'n I were too young to make a dent, so we were practically eatin' our legs. I was the youngest, y'know? n' sometimes I really thought my brothers were gonna' come after me.

ERNIE: Whata' y'mean?

MIKE: You know.

ERNIE: What, like try to eat ya'?

MIKE: Yeah, man. I didn't know.

ERNIE: *(Guffaws...)* You are so fulla' shit, my friend....

MIKE: *(Over "my friend...")* Ern, I'm tellin' ya', for a few years, it was like Lord a' the fuckin' Flies in my house. But no matter how broke we were,...she could always give $20 to that fuckin' fake nun. So there y'go. That's my mother.

> *(A moment, as they eat, while Ernie tries to contain his amusement...)*

ERNIE: n'yet you still live with 'er.

MIKE: Don't remind me.

ERNIE: Well, c'mon now, you can be on your own.

MIKE: Ernie, I know...

ERNIE: Been here almost 2 years.

MIKE: Yeah...

ERNIE: Got enough for a 1st'n last months, right?

MIKE: Yeah, yeah…

ERNIE: Gotta' stop bein' lazy.

MIKE: I know.

ERNIE: Shit, how can y'date a girl when y'live with your mama.

MIKE: Don't ask.

ERNIE: Right. Can't even have her over with your mom in the next room with a glass to the wall.

MIKE: I've tried.

ERNIE: I know.

MIKE: Wasn't pretty.

ERNIE: She walked in on ya' once, right?

MIKE: Once?

ERNIE: More than once?

MIKE: *(Grinning…)* Ernie…

ERNIE: How many times?

MIKE: Enough t'make me wana' consider the fuckin' priest-hood, okay?

ERNIE: Y'see that ain't right.

MIKE: Alright, so I go t'*their* houses.

ERNIE: Yeah, but y'wana be a host in a place y'can call your own. That's what it's about.

MIKE: Yeah, but if I'm at *their* place, I got an excuse to leave.

ERNIE: Are you f'real?

MIKE: *(Laughs…)* What?

ERNIE: I thought you wanted t'get married someday.

MIKE: Yeah, *some*day. Not today.

ERNIE: Well, you got many more days t'go with that philosophy.

MIKE: I know.

ERNIE: C'mon now.

MIKE: I'm an idiot that way. Whata' y'want…?

ERNIE: You ain't dumb or I wouldn't waste my time on ya'.

MIKE: Good at my job, shitty in every other way.

ERNIE: Well, listen t'me.

MIKE: I do.

ERNIE: No, don't jus' nod'n eat your salami sandwich. Listen'n absorb, man. Y'snap your fingers n'you're practically a senior citizen. That's how life works. You put off'n you put off'n you put off, n'before you know it, you're gray-haired, with no teeth, in a room alone n'playin' that digital candy game into your Golden years, n'not even knowin' what the sky looks like anymore.

MIKE: Holy shit.

ERNIE: What?

MIKE: Ernie, you should like totally speak to junior high school classes or somethin'. You'd scare them straight.

ERNIE: They don't have the attention-span t'be scared.

(MIKE laughs, as if familiar terrain…)

You think I'm jokin'? In 10 years, a complete sentence will a' gone the way of the West African Black Rhino. Mark my words.

MIKE: Here we go.

ERNIE: Eulogies n'graduate speeches'll be reduced to fuckin' acronyms.

MIKE: Alright, Ern…

ERNIE: A president's inaugural address'll come down to nothin' but an LOL and a standin' ovation, before everybody goes back to their lil' digital-doodads.

MIKE: Okay, got ya'…

ERNIE: But there's hope for you. You got eyes'n ears.

MIKE: I know.

ERNIE: Get a place a' your own.

MIKE: I will.

ERNIE: Get y'self a nice girl.

MIKE: I got a girl.

ERNIE: Yeah, but she nice?

MIKE: Is she nice? What, do I wanna' marry her? No.

ERNIE: You've never even mentioned her by name.

MIKE: Well, it's casual. I haven't had a reason to mention her name, Ern.

ERNIE: How long you with 'er?

MIKE: Jus' a few months.

ERNIE: You *know* her name?

MIKE: *(Nearly chokes on drink...)* Yeah, I know 'er name.

ERNIE: What is it?

MIKE: Darlene, okay?

ERNIE: Darlene.

MIKE: n'Karen.

ERNIE: You datin' two girls or does Darlene have a split personality?

MIKE: I jus' met Karen at a club a coupla' weeks ago.

ERNIE: Uh-huh.

MIKE: Ern, it's not serious. Either of 'em. Very casual.

ERNIE: Uh-huh.

MIKE: That's it.

ERNIE: Do *they* know this?

MIKE: They know what they know. I dunno, Ern. It's not like
we've done the Bed'n Breakfast trips or whatever. It's grabbin' a
burger, foolin' around... That kinda' stuff. There's no...long
term whatever-the-hell.

ERNIE: Okay.

MIKE: At least I don't think. I dunno'. I guess the less I know
the better right now. Y'know?

ERNIE: Alright. *(...as he takes a bite...)*

MIKE: Y'don't think that makes me a shit or somethin', do ya'?

ERNIE: C'mon. Hell, I was young once. Like to think I'm young t'day but I'd be a lyin' sack a shit.

MIKE: You're not old, Ern.

ERNIE: I didn't say I was old, jus' said I wasn't young.

MIKE: Alright, sorry.

ERNIE: Have fun, jus' don't get lost in it, y'know?

MIKE: Yeah, I know.

ERNIE: n'don't hurt nobody.

MIKE: Yeah, I hear ya'.

ERNIE: There's no book to this shit. I mean, God knows I know enough people who've already married'n divorced three'n four times over, jus' cause that's what's been drilled into 'em. Then they get married again as if jus' to say they are, while they cryin' themselves to sleep.

MIKE: Gimme a fuckin' break...

ERNIE: Better off stayin' single n'gettin' a turtle or somethin'. Be a lot cheaper.

MIKE: Exactly.

ERNIE: There y'go.

MIKE: Like my brotha'. I told you about him.

ERNIE: Which one? Vinnie or Joey?

MIKE: Well, they're both fuckin' idiots, but Vinnie. The oldest. I look at him n' I'm like, "Why?" He's fuckin' in hell, n'yet anytime I see 'im it's always *"Grow up'n get married"*. What, like *him*? Ern, they've had the cops over their house I don't know how many times 'cause they can't talk to each other without fuckin' primal screaming. Yet when he sees me, and he's yellin' at her across the house, he's still givin' me shit for not havin' my own family.

ERNIE: *There's* incentive.

MIKE: Right?

ERNIE: I hear ya'.

MIKE: I mean, shit…

ERNIE: You'll figure it out for y'self.

MIKE: Yeah, I know.

ERNIE: It's not about doin' what everybody else does. In the end, it's about doin' somethin' that means somethin' to ya'. Whatever that is'n however you get there is up to you – as long as you get there. Road less traveled, all that.

MIKE: Yeah.

ERNIE: But you still need t'get outa' that house.

MIKE: I know.

ERNIE: I'm serious now.

MIKE: Ern, I will. I'm halfway out the door.

(A moment, as they eat…)

MIKE: That's from somethin', right?

ERNIE: What?

MIKE: "The road less traveled". Who said that?

ERNIE: Frost.

MIKE: Who?

ERNIE: Robert Frost. It's from a poem a' his.

MIKE: Called *The Road Less Travelled*?

ERNIE: *The Road Not Taken.*

MIKE: Wait, *The Road Less Travelled* is *The Road Not Taken*?

ERNIE: There is no *Road Less Travelled*. The poem is called *The Road Not Taken*. "The Road Less Travelled" is a line from the poem called, *The Road Not Taken*...

MIKE: *(with "The Road Not Taken"...) ...The Road Not Taken.*

ERNIE: Give the man a pickle.

> *(ERNIE hands MIKE the wrapped pickle from his lunch, as JOSE enters...)*

JOSE: Ernie, Mike, you still at lunch?

ERNIE: We still eatin' ain't we?

JOSE: Jus' heard from Javier's wife. She said the surgery went okay.

ERNIE: Good t'hear.

JOSE: Bed rest for a while, n'then it looks like he'll be goin' on disability.

MIKE: Figured.

ERNIE: Guy drinks'n smokes like a fish breathes through its lungs. He's lucky t'be alive.

JOSE: I been tellin' 'im.

ERNIE: First month on this job, n'the sonofabitch keels over like a condemned building.

JOSE: In the ambulance, he was even askin' the fuckin' EMS workers for a smoke.

ERNIE: Unbelievable.

JOSE: So now we got this new guy comin', right?

ERNIE: Yeah, t'morrow.

JOSE: Y'think that's gonna' help us or hurt us?

ERNIE: They said he knew his shit, so we'll see. If he's as experienced as they say, we shouldn't have t'hold his hand too much.

JOSE: I dunno, man.

ERNIE: You don't know what? We don't have a choice.

JOSE: They been up our ass with this one, y'know?

ERNIE: Yeah, I know.

JOSE: They want this shit done by the fall.

ERNIE: Yeah, I know.

JOSE: Six months, Ern.

ERNIE: I know.

JOSE: So why they sendin' us someone new?

ERNIE: Because Javier went'n had a damn heart attack, 'at's why.

JOSE: They don't think we're slackin'?

ERNIE: What the hell you mean? If they thought we were slackin', they wouldn't be sendin' us a new guy.

JOSE: Y'sure?

ERNIE: Yeah, I'm sure. We're equipped to move a new guy along without skippin' a beat, n'they know it. n'he's s'pposed t'be a good one, t'boot. Practically a foreman, where he used t'be. They jus' want us to have a full crew.

MIKE: But that's a good point. Why *are* they up our ass with this one, Ern?

JOSE: It's a dedication park.

MIKE: Yeah, I know that, Jose. But why're they tryin' to rush it? They already clipped two months off our timeline.

ERNIE: Because it's an election year, and this is a very important park. That's why.

MIKE: What?!

JOSE: But there's weather issues they gotta' take into account.

ERNIE: I know.

JOSE: Rain, sleet, snow...

ERNIE: Yes, I know what weather is.

JOSE: I'm jus' sayin' we can't control that. Mama Nature's got a mind a' her own, y'know...?

ERNIE: I know, Jose, but they're bettering their odds by makin' sure we got enough manpower. Someone else can go down, who

21

knows. The way you eat, you may be in a gurney right alongside Javier before y'know it. That's business'n that's politics. I don't question it. I jus' do my job n'make sure everyone else is doin' theirs so that we can get this thing done. Now will you let us finish our damn lunch, please?

JOSE: Alright, alright. Sorry,...

ERNIE: I didn't talk shop to you while you were droppin' that rancid-lookin' meatball sandwich all over your overalls. Damn...

JOSE: *(Over "Damn...")* Alright, sorry. I'll let you guys finish.

MIKE/ERNIE: Thank you.

JOSE: Mike, you gonna' eat that pickle.

MIKE: Here. It's Ernie's.

JOSE: Thanks, Ern.

MIKE: But he gave it t'*me*.

JOSE: *(As he bites pickle...)* Thanks, Mike.

(JOSE exits... As ERNIE and MIKE finish up...)

ERNIE: As stressed as he is, the motherfucker can always eat.

MIKE: Tsch, no fuckin' wonder.

ERNIE: What?

MIKE: I didn't connect why they've been on us so much about this one until you jus' said it.

ERNIE: I thought you knew.

MIKE: How would I know? They don't tell ya'.

ERNIE: Of course not.

MIKE: See, that's why I don't vote.

ERNIE: You don't vote?

MIKE: No.

ERNIE: Whata' y'mean y'don't vote? Y'gotta' vote.

MIKE: Why, f'this kinda' bullshit?

ERNIE: The park ain't bullshit. The reason they're bustin' our chops is.

MIKE: That's what I'm sayin', Ern. People got fuckin' killed here, and to that prick it's a fuckin' photo op.

ERNIE: You still gotta' vote.

MIKE: No way, Ern.

ERNIE: Get outa' that house n'register t'vote. That's your t'do list, y'understand?

MIKE: That's my list.

ERNIE: That's a start.

MIKE: C'mon, Ern, I'm gonna' vote jus' so I can be out-voted?

ERNIE: You didn't even vote yet? What makes you think you gonna' be out-voted?

MIKE: 'cause I never like the guy who gets in.

ERNIE: Oh, Jesus...

MIKE: What...?

ERNIE: That's the excuse a' every motherfucker who doesn't vote. Why bother, right?

MIKE: It's a *good* excuse.

ERNIE: Look, y'vote, you got an argument for who's in. You don't, you got no one t'blame but y'self.

MIKE: Yeah, myself and the ones who voted.

ERNIE: And the ones who didn't vote at all.

MIKE: Right, so why bother?

ERNIE: 'cause if no one votes then, before y'know it, our Mayor's a fake nun with a teak salad bowl! That's why. Register to fuckin' vote. Now we're done with the political segment. You gonna' eat your chips?

MIKE: *(Rolls eyes, with a grin...)* No, finish 'em.

> *(They sit with their gathered lunch garbage, as ERNIE finishes MIKE's chips...)*

> *(A moment.)*

MIKE: Hard to believe you don't have kids.

ERNIE: Why d'ya' say that?

MIKE: Why? C'mon, the way you bust balls. Jesus Christ, you're a natural.

ERNIE: Well, what can I tell ya'. I guess you bring it out in me, Mike.

MIKE: Tsch...

ERNIE: How are we on time?

MIKE: Like 5 'til.

(A moment.)

Shit, why ain't *you* married?

ERNIE: I *was* married.

MIKE: I mean, now. You should be married now.

ERNIE: Why now?

MIKE: What? Jus'…you'd make a good husband, I bet.

ERNIE: You proposin'?

MIKE: Kiss my ass. I'm serious.

ERNIE: *(Slight pause, eating…)* Not the way things worked out.

MIKE: You ever thoughta' gettin' hitched again?

ERNIE: *(Slight pause.)* I did.

MIKE: *(Slight pause.)* No?

ERNIE: *(Slight pause, closes his eyes, with a subtle smile…)*

> *I shall be telling this with a sigh*
> *Somewhere ages and ages hence:*
> *Two roads diverged in a wood, and I—*
> *I took the one less traveled by,*
> *And that has made all the difference.*

(A moment. They look at each other.)

MIKE: *The Road Not Taken?*

ERNIE: Give that man another pickle.

> *(ERNIE pulls out a second pickle from his lunch…)*

25

(Lights)

Scene 2

*About a week later. SAM, MIKE and ERNIE at lunch on site –
mid-laughter…*

MIKE: …Two fuckin' Butterballs, man!

ERNIE: *(Under "Butterballs…")* God as my witness…

SAM: Jesus Christ…

MIKE: n'the way she tried t'play it off, right?

SAM: Holdin' 'em like her kids.

ERNIE: Well, what else could she do, right? There wasn't another stop for like 10 blocks…

SAM: Yeah, right. What, she gonna' hop out like James Bond
or somethin'…?

MIKE: Do a drop'n roll on the street with two turkeys in 'er
hand.

(They laugh…)

ERNIE: Never been able to look at a pregnant woman the same
way since, man…

SAM: Sure, who could blame ya'?

MIKE: I told Ern he should give 'em a questionnaire before
givin' up his seat next time.

ERNIE: Ask 'em how many months,…

MIKE: Get her husband's name,…

ERNIE: Her obstetrician's.

> *(They laugh…)*

ERNIE: Hey, if all a scam artist gets from me is a seat on the bus, I'll consider myself fortunate.

SAM: I hear ya'.

ERNIE: I'll take fakin' pregnancy'n stealin' turkeys over some Madoff bullshit any day.

> *(They laugh…)*

SAM: Shit, one time I'm comin' into the city. This was years ago. I was still in Brooklyn at the time.

MIKE: 'k.

SAM: This guy gets on - on crutches, okay?

ERNIE: Oh, here we go.

SAM: On crutches.

MIKE: Yeah.

SAM: He's writhing in pain like a wounded animal with like a Srilankan accent or somethin'.

ERNIE: Srilanka?

SAM: Yeah, around there somewhere. So he gets on, amblin' along with these crutches, n'all he can say is 4 words – *"Hungry – Thirsty – Hernia – Operation"*.

MIKE: Hah!   /   ERNIE: Okay.

SAM: That's all he can say, with this thick accent *(with accent)* – *"Hungry – Thirsty – Hernia – Operation"*. So we're all watchin' this guy draggin' himself through the fuckin' car with this empty Pringle's can in his hand, right? n'he's squealin' - *"Hungry – Thirsty – Hernia – Operation – Hungry – Thirst – Hernia – Operation"*. I get t'my stop, Union Square, n'I gotta' transfer to the uptown 6. n'I'm in a hurry too, okay? So I bolt up two flights a' stairs, hop on the 6 just as the fuckin' doors close, all within less than 3 minutes time. I sit down in the car, still tryin' t'catch my breath, the door to the previous car opens, n'I hear - *"Hungry – Thirsty – Hernia – Operation…"*

(Mike & Ernie laugh over "Thirsty…")

MIKE: Oh, shit…!   /   ERNIE: Saw it comin', saw it
                                         comin'…

SAM: The guy could barely walk n'he made it up 2 flights in under 3 minutes without breakin' a fuckin' sweat.

ERNIE: n'went right into his spiel.

SAM: n'I'm still pantin'. Guy was in better shape than I was, f'Godsakes.

MIKE: Funny fuckin' shit…

ERNIE: Damn if I can find the woodwork they come out of, man…

SAM: Right?

(The laugh peters, as they eat, drink…)

ERNIE: You in Astoria now, y'said?

SAM: Yeah, jus' moved a few months ago.

ERNIE: Nice over there.

SAM: Yeah, it's okay.

MIKE: You near the Greeks?

SAM: Yeah, Ditmars Blvd.

ERNIE: Fuckin' good restaurants.

SAM: Yep.

ERNIE: Mike, you got one a' your ladies there too, right?

MIKE: Yeah, Astoria Blvd.

SAM: *One* of 'em. Look a' this guy.

MIKE: Nah, nah…

ERNIE: Oh, yeah.

MIKE: Ern, c'mon…

ERNIE: What, I didn't say y'had a harem, f'cryin' out loud.

SAM: How many?

MIKE: Two, that's it.

SAM: Hey, it's one more than one, man. Enjoy it while y'can.

MIKE: Yeah, thanks.

ERNIE: How long y'married. Sam?

SAM: Well,…I *was* married 16 years.

ERNIE: Oh. Y'said wife the other day, so I thought…

SAM: We're separated.

ERNIE: Oh, I hear ya'.

SAM: Not in the habit a' sayin' ex yet, so that's why, y'know?

ERNIE: Sure.

MIKE: *(Slight pause, bites…)* 16 years.

SAM: Yep.

ERNIE: Two kids, y'said?

SAM: Yeah, 12'n 10.

ERNIE: *(Slight pause, as he eats…)* Tough age for that kinda stuff.

SAM: Yeah, y'know, old enough t'know too much, n'not old enough t'know how t'handle it.

MIKE: Yeah, shit.

ERNIE: Well, sorry you gotta' go through it.

MIKE: Yeah, man. That's fucked up.

SAM: Hey, whata' y'gonna' do. It is what it is.

(A moment, as they eat, drink...)

SAM: What about you, Ern? How long y'married?

ERNIE: I'm not. I was.

SAM: Divorced?

ERNIE: My wife died.

SAM: Oh. Shit.

ERNIE: Long time ago.

SAM: Sorry t'hear that.

ERNIE: Well, like y'said, it is what it is. Sometimes it's a *sad* is, y'know?

(A moment, as they eat...)

MIKE: Ern's a poet, Sam.

SAM: Yeah?

MIKE: Yeah, he writes poems. / ERNIE: Mike,...

SAM: 'at's cool.

ERNIE: Don't go by him, Sam.

MIKE: Whata' y'mean don't go by me...?

ERNIE: He ain't even heard 'em.

MIKE: That's because you won't lemme hear 'em.

ERNIE: You still ain't heard 'em.

MIKE: How many times I asked ya' t'let me hear 'em or read 'em – nothin'.

ERNIE: I told ya' I'd let ya' hear somethin' someday.

MIKE: What day? It's been over a fuckin' year, Ern!

ERNIE: *(to Sam)* It's mainly somethin' I do for myself, that's all.

MIKE: But you hear how he talks, right? You can tell he's good.

ERNIE: What the hella' you doin', tryin' t'make a black man blush, f'Godsakes?!

MIKE: I'm saying I know you're good without knowin' it.

ERNIE: I think you're anglin' for my potato salad. That's what I think.

MIKE: I don't want your… Sam, he quotes from other guys all the time. Have you heard 'em?

SAM: No,…

MIKE: Yeah, like fuckin' Hemingway, Poe. Who was that guy from last week? Frost?

ERNIE: Robert Frost.

MIKE: Robert Frost – *The Road Not Taken.* Y'know that one?

SAM: No, I…

MIKE: He jus' closes his eyes n'recites it like he's on the fuckin' stage or somethin'. Who does that?

ERNIE: People do it.

MIKE: *You* do it. I don't know people who do that.

SAM: Neither do I.

MIKE: Fuck, I don't know people who can *read* let alone fuckin' recite Robert Frost. Are you kiddin' me? I mention Robert Frost t'someone in my neighborhood, they think it's what nips at ya' nose at Christmas.

SAM: That's cool, Ern. You should bring in some a' your poems sometime.

ERNIE: Yeah, we'll see.

MIKE: You heard back about the one you submitted for the park?

ERNIE: No, not yet.

SAM: What's 'is?

MIKE: Ern submitted a poem to recite at the ribbon cutting when the park opens.

SAM: One you wrote?

ERNIE: It's a long shot.

MIKE: Hey, y'never know, man.

ERNIE: I just' got the urge to write somethin' back when they announced funding for it. I'm still workin' on it, but I sent 'em a draft a coupla' months back, so we'll see what they say.

SAM: What's it called?

ERNIE: Well, I wanted to name it after the park, but they don't have a name yet, so right now it's jus' called *Dedication*.

SAM: Well, good luck, man.

MIKE: Cool, huh?

ERNIE: I jus' submitted it, Mike, 'at's all.

MIKE: Yeah, n' if they know their ass from their balls, they'll select it.

ERNIE: Whether they know that or not, n'I think they should, it don't mean they'll pick it.

MIKE: I know.

ERNIE: Look, I think I'm as I should be about it, y'know? That's how y'gotta' be about things outa' your hands. A cautious optimist with a half-empty glass.

MIKE: Y'see, Sam?

SAM: See what?

MIKE: How he does a spin on the glass-half full thing…

ERNIE: Here's my potato salad. Now shut the hell up.

MIKE: Kiss my ass. How can they not pick it?

ERNIE: They can *not* pick it.

MIKE: C'mon, y'got talent. You're almost a 20-year vet of the parks department...

ERNIE: You think that means dick on a stick to them? They'll be havin' all these speakers, the mayor, borough president...

MIKE: You got more to say than all those dipshits.

ERNIE: Even still.

MIKE: Those douchebags need to speak less and let guys like you talk.

ERNIE: Alright, well, we'll see what happens. *(Takes a bite...)* But I appreciate it, okay?

MIKE: *Now* I'll take the potato salad.

ERNIE: What, *all* of it?

MIKE: No, jus' give me like two spoonfuls. This is your home-made, right?

ERNIE: Of course. Our insurance ain't good enough for me to get it from around here.

MIKE: Yeah, no shit.

> *(Ernie spoons potato salad into Mike's tupperware container...)*

> *(A moment, as they eat, drink...)*

SAM: My daughter has a... She likes to write.

ERNIE: Oh, yeah?

SAM: Yeah.

ERNIE: What kinda' stuff?

SAM: Mainly short little songs n'stuff.

MIKE: Cool.

SAM: She wrote a children's story too.

ERNIE: Yeah?

SAM: Yeah.

ERNIE: About what?

SAM: A rappin' rhinoceros.

ERNIE: A rappin' what?

MIKE: Rhinoceros?

SAM: Yeah.

MIKE: That's awesome.

SAM: Yeah, it's…it's a cute little story.

ERNIE: What's the story?

SAM: Well, he's… He's this rappin' rhino who's like always in a good mood n' he raps to sad people t'cheer 'em up.

MIKE: Cool.

ERNIE: Very cute.

SAM: They're not even people, mainly. Animals, reptiles...
Like a turtle, raccoon...

ERNIE: Yeah, okay.

SAM: The last one is a person. The last one he raps to. A man.
She said it's me.

ERNIE: You're in the book. Look a' that.

SAM: *(Slight pause.)* Yeah. The rhino's tryin' to cheer me up.

ERNIE: *(Slight pause.)* Hm.

> *(A moment, as they eat, as Sam sits with this thought, which Ernie and Mike pick up on...)*

ERNIE: You're doin' good work, Sam. Y'don't get rich workin' for the city, but it's gratifying jus' the same, y'know? You'll be a good fit.

MIKE: Yeah, man.

SAM: Thanks, guys. Appreciate it.

JOSE: *(Offstage...)* Ernie?!

ERNIE: Que pasa, mi amigo loco?

> *(JOSE enters...)*

JOSE: You think we'll be able to lay down the fabric today?

ERNIE: Yeah, if it don't rain.   Otherwise, we'll be puttin' down the tarp.

JOSE: Whata' y'think?

ERNIE: What you mean, what I think?   It ain't rainin' yet, so let's jus' see. The water ain't gonna' damage anything.   Hell, the rocks are out, so it'll be good they get another cleanin'.

JOSE: But we already cleaned 'em.

ERNIE: It's water, Jose. There is no greater friend to a rock than water. Water jus' slides off like a duck's back without the quack.

JOSE: Alright.

ERNIE: Hey, how about Sam, huh?

JOSE: What?

ERNIE: A week in, I think we can safely say he's workin' out, right?

JOSE: Yeah, yeah. He is. Good job, Sam.

SAM: Thanks, man.

ERNIE: Man knows 'is stuff.

SAM: Jus' doin' my job, but thanks, man.

MIKE: Hey, we even picked up a step.

JOSE: I'm still tryin' to figure out if we met before.

SAM: *(Smiles...)* Yeah, ya' mentioned that.

ERNIE: It's New York, Jose. Everyone looks like someone.

JOSE: I know, but it's annoyin' when you think you met someone n'can't place 'im.

MIKE: Sam, does Jose look familiar?

SAM: Not really.

MIKE: Alright, so there's half the problem solved.

JOSE: How does 'at solve anything?

MIKE: He looks familiar to you but you don't t'him.

JOSE: Yeah, so?

MIKE: So maybe you never met each other but you met someone who looks like 'im.

JOSE: Or maybe we met n'he doesn't remember me.

ERNIE: Who could not remember you? If I met you once, you'd still be in my nightmares.

(They laugh, even Jose…)

JOSE: You kid 'cause you love, right, Ern…?

ERNIE: There y'go…

JOSE: Whass 'at?

MIKE: What?

JOSE: That. That Ernie's potato salad?

MIKE: Yeah.

ERNIE: I swear you gotta' tapeworm. Didn't you jus' eat?

JOSE: Whata' y'want, I got 6 friggin' kids'n they're eatin' me outa' house'n home. I gotta' make up for it when I'm here.

ERNIE: Alright, here take the resta' my damn potato salad, n'gimme back the tupperware when you're done, y'hear?

JOSE: Alright, gracias.

ERNIE: Denada.

> *(JOSE exits, while scarfing potato salad... As Mike and Ernie chuckle...)*

ERNIE: Pieca' work, right?

SAM: Yeah.

ERNIE: He's a good guy. Jus' gets a little too stressed some-times.

MIKE: Jus' give 'em your lunch n' that usually shuts 'im up for a bit.

SAM: Yeah, you guys seem t'have a system.

ERNIE: We started workin' together over 10 years ago. First job together was re-seeding the garden up near Hunt's Point. Felt the same as I do now; good guy, good worker, but a pain in my God-damn ass. But then it was jus' inexperience. Now it's experience n'neurosis. Like a Puerto Rican Woody Allen.

> *(They laugh...)*

SAM: Yeah, I've worked with guys like him before.

ERNIE: Yeah, you worked out on the Island, y'said?

SAM: Yeah. Farmington, thereabouts.

MIKE: How was 'at?

SAM: Served its purpose, y'know? Cut my teeth. When I started there, it was literally the owner'n two guys under 'em.

MIKE: Shit, that's mom'n pop.

SAM: Yeah, it started that way, but not so much when I left. Once he realized I knew what I was doin', he had me supervisin' the other two. That freed him up to drum up more business, so as he got more customers, he needed more guys. By the time I left, I was overseein' 25 workers, n'trained 'em all too.

ERNIE: Yeah, heard y'knew your shit.

MIKE: How long were y'there?

SAM: About 6 years.

MIKE: Why'd y'leave?

SAM: Eh, y'know,…limitations.

ERNIE: Sounds like he was really expandin' though.

SAM: Yeah, well, jus' cause you do more business don't neces-sarily mean you make more money.

MIKE: So what, y'jus' left?

SAM: Well, I tried t'start my own thing.

MIKE: Your own business?

SAM: Yeah. Knew all the ropes, made some contacts, I thought but… Eh, it didn't work out too well.

MIKE: How come, y'think?

ERNIE: Mike.

MIKE: What?

ERNIE: Askin' a man why his business didn't succeed's like askin' 'im why he shits at night.

MIKE: What, Ern? I'm jus…

SAM: No, it's cool, Ern. It was a lota' factors, Mike.

MIKE: Like what?

ERNIE: Mike, Sam doesn't gotta' give us his whole life story in one lunch, so…

MIKE: I'm jus' askin'. I thought maybe in a few years, I might start my own thing, so I'm jus' curious.

SAM: Well, in that case, I'll tell ya' this; make sure y'got reliable backers if you're not startin' with your own money.

MIKE: You had backers?

SAM: *(Slight pause.)* Thought I did. Had people that said they'd be there for me n'when I looked for 'em, they may as well a' been in the witness protection program. So there y'go.

MIKE: That fuckin' sucks.

SAM: Yeah. It did.

(SAM takes a bite out of his sandwich, gazes out, as MIKE and ERNIE pick up on this, as earlier...)

ERNIE: Y'know, lived in New York all my life, n'I don't think I've been on the Island but twice.   One time was a fishin' trip with a buddy out in Montauk and then the other was seein' Stevie Wonder at Jones Beach.

MIKE: Stevie Wonder? Jesus, when was this?

ERNIE: Hey, don't be knockin' Stevie.

MIKE: I'm not. Jus' askin'.

ERNIE: Like 25 years ago.

MIKE: Yeah, 'at sounds about right.

ERNIE: *(Elbows Mike...)* Y'know I can still bury you under the mulch, my friend...

MIKE: *(Laughs...)* Alright, alright.... Hey, Sam, I may still pick y'brain sometime, if ya' don't mind, okay?

SAM: About what?

MIKE: About startin' your own business. Shit, y'still got more experience than me.

SAM: Uh, ...yeah, sure, man.

MIKE: Ern'll tell ya', I didn't know shit when I started here.

ERNIE: n'now I can proudly say he knows shit.

MIKE: I'm jus' thinkin' a few years up the road, who knows.

ERNIE: World's your oyster. I always tell ya'.

MIKE: Not in a rush though. I like workin' for the city, y'know?
There's somethin' nice about workin' on stuff that like hundreds
a' people'll see at some point. I think that's kinda' cool.

SAM: Sure, yeah.

ERNIE: This park should get some traffic.

MIKE: Hopefully the right kind.

SAM: You ain't kiddin. I remember this 'hood from years ago.
It's like frozen in time.

MIKE: Never even knew this was here before. What the hell
were *you* doin' here?

SAM: Y'know, jus'…drivin' through. Who remembers? Jus'
remember it bein' a hole.

ERNIE: Never had reason to be here m'self, n'I've been in
Queens 35 years now. Never even heard of this area until I read
about what happened.

SAM: Yeah, so what actually happened here? All I know is
two kids got killed.

MIKE: s'fucked up.

ERNIE: *(Swallows…)* Two girls. One black, one white. They
were shortcuttin' through here when it was jus' an abandoned

parking lot. They were headin' to the train. The white girl was at the black girl's house, tutoring each other for the damn SATs. That somethin'? Was gettin' late, black girl didn't want the white one goin' to the train by herself, so she went with 'er. They're comin' through the parking lot, they end up gettin' stopped by 4 punks who raped 'em both, stabbed 'em a bunch a' times n'left 'em for dead no more than 100 feet from where we are.

MIKE: *(With mouthful…)* Fucked up, right?

SAM: Yeah. I guess I musta' heard about it but it got lost in all the other bad shit y'hear about.

MIKE: I can see why she'd wana' walk with her too. This place's fuckin' rough, man.

ERNIE: Not much different than where I grew up in the Bronx, I'll tell ya'. Always thought that was half the problem with a lota' these neighborhoods, y'know? If they jus' had more places t'go instead jus' bodegas or hangin' out in the street. *(Slight pause.)* I mean, y'got some people, they don't know what the fuck t'do around here. They don't work or they're outa' work for whatever reason. They walk the same blocks, they don't take the train anywhere else, go into the city, go to Central Park jus' to breathe different air. I mean, man, I grew up in a fuckin' war zone but I tell ya', I loved comin' to the city, with whatever nickels'n dimes I had. Goin' to the Vanguard, Fillmore East, Blue Note… Museums, seein' movies'n shit. But a lot never leave. Like here. They jus' stay. For generations, even. They stay, they hang out, they drink, smoke weed, they fuck around. n'the people that know better are afraid to leave the house 'cause they feel, if they do, what'll happen to them'll be what happened to those two girls. So they either live in fear or fear livin'. *(Slight pause.)* But y'hope, hey, maybe this'll be the start a' somethin' nice here, y'know?

SAM: *(A beat, skeptically looking at the surroundings...)* Y'hope.

MIKE: *(The same...)* I dunno', Ern.

ERNIE: *(Slight pause, last bite.)* Gotta' be optimistic, or else what the hell we doin' this for, right?

> *(As ERNIE rises, gathers his trash...)*

ERNIE: Alright, fellas. Guess we should try'n get as much as we can in before the rain comes.

MIKE: Yep.

ERNIE: Gonna' hit the head.

> *(ERNIE dumps trash in garbage can, exits, as MIKE and SAM gather their trash...)*

MIKE: Hey, man, since we been workin' here, we sometimes go knock one back at that skeezy lookin' place by the train.

SAM: Yeah?

MIKE: Grubby's or Gruffy's or some shit? It's a shithole but the mugs're at least clean.

SAM: Okay.

MIKE: Anyway, we usually go after work on Fridays, jus' so y'know.

SAM: Cool, thanks, man. Yeah, sounds like a plan.

> *(SAM takes Mike's trash., along with his...)*

SAM: Here, I got it…

MIKE: Thanks.

(SAM walks to trash, with a subtle but noticeable limp…)

MIKE: You okay?

SAM: What?

MIKE: Pull a hammy or somethin'?

SAM: Nah, old injury. Comes'n goes, y'know?

MIKE: Jus' take it easy liftin' the sandbags, man. Don't wana' make it worse.

SAM: It's cool.

MIKE: We're a crew, y'know. Jus' ask if ya' need help.

SAM: Hey, lemme know whenever you wana' talk about startin' up a business. I didn't do too well myself, obviously, but…y'know, I can still give ya' some tips. Jus' lemme know.

MIKE: Yeah, thanks, man. I'll take ya' up on that.

(SAM dumps everything in can…)

So what'd you do before landscapin'?

SAM: Whata' y'mean?

MIKE: Y'said you cut your teeth out on the Island.

SAM: Yeah.

MIKE: That means y'did somethin' before, right?

SAM: *(With a snicker.)* Whata' you, a ladies man *and* a detective?

MIKE: Hah. You laugh, but I actually wanted t'be a cop at one point.

SAM: Yeah? What happened?

MIKE: Whata' y'think? I was a fuckin' pussy. Didn't wana' get killed.

SAM: Nah, that don't make you a pussy.

MIKE: Whatever. I didn't become a cop, okay?

SAM: Yeah, well, I wouldn't beat yourself up. There's other ways a' makin' a living.

    (...as he starts off...)

MIKE: Yeah, I know. So what'd you do before?

SAM: *(Slight pause, laughs.)* Boy, you don't let up, do ya'?

MIKE: Sorry, man, jus' makin' conversation.. You don't have to… If it's personal…

SAM*: (Slight pause.)* I was a cop, Mike.

MIKE: *(A beat.)* What?!

SAM: Mike, listen…

MIKE: No shit…?

SAM: Mike, I really don't wana' make a thing about it, okay?

MIKE: Why? That's fuckin' cool, man…

SAM: *(over "cool, man…")* Yeah, but I jus'…y'know, I don't want anybodin' knowin'.

MIKE: Why, man…?

SAM: *(Over "man…")* It was another part a' my life n'it's done, that's all, okay? I jus' wana' be one a' the guys here. Seriously.

MIKE: *(A beat.)* Alri…yeah, that's cool.

SAM: Not even Ernie, okay? I'm serious.

MIKE: *(Slight pause.)* Yeah, okay.

SAM: Thanks, man. Really. *(He pats Mike on shoulder…)* Hey, it's good workin' with a fellow Brooklynite. It's been a while, y'know?

MIKE: Yeah, man. Back at ya'.

> *(SAM walks off with his subtle limp, as MIKE watches him, then snaps out of it.)*

MIKE: *(Calling off…)* HEY, ERN, WE'RE BACK, OKAY?!

> *(Lights, sound of rain, distant thunder…)*

Scene 3

Friday evening, after a shift. ERNIE, MIKE and SAM at table, at bar. Several empty beer mugs and glasses are strewn about, and chairs from other departed workers… Laughter abounds…

ERNIE: ...Man, I'm tellin' ya' whenever I did shit as a kid, n'I did some crazy-ass shit, my father always gave what he called "The Two Options".

MIKE: Oh, fuck...

ERNIE: He said *"Now I can beat ya' good or I can beat ya' bad."*

SAM: Shit, they both sound pretty bad t'me...

MIKE: *(Over "bad t'me...")* What the fuck was the difference...?

ERNIE: Well, wait now... Beat ya' bad meant he'd use a belt, n'beat ya' good meant he'd use his hand.

SAM: Fist?

ERNIE: Nah, open hand. But it was still a big black thick callused fuckin' catcher's glove of a motherfuckin' hand, okay? n'he worked on a factory line at a can company his whole life, so he had cuts'n scrapes'n shit. It was like gettin' spanked with a brick covered with sandpaper. But that was still better than the belt. So whenever he gave me "the two options", I always said, *"I'll take the good"* – n'he'd gimme 5 across the behind with his big ol' fat hand, n'that was 'at. Well, coupla' years later, my father'd passed, n'I was even worse, man. Actin' out, gettin' into shit, skippin' school... n'my mother had had enough. Never laid a reprimandin' hand on me her whole life, but that was it. So one day I'd gotten into some shit, n'she grabs a hold a' me n'says, *"Your father may not be here anymore, but I can still give ya' what for."* n'she gives me the two options...

MIKE: Fuckin' shit... / SAM: That's fuckin' funny...

ERNIE: n'she did it jus' like him, *"I can beat ya' bad or beat ya' good."* So, of course, I'm thinkin' a' my mom's little soft creamy hands. So if there's one thing I knew, is that I'd take the good over the bad. So I said, *"Alright, I'll take the good"* – WHACK! Right across my ass with the belt!

MIKE/SAM: HAH!!!!

ERNIE: Not jus' a belt now, okay? A thick leather rhinestone studded belt that left welts on my ass for the next three goddamn months, alright?

MIKE: Fuckin' shit…

ERNIE: So I turn to my mother, with tears in my eyes, n'said *"What the hell you doin'? You supposed to use your hand?"* n'she said, *"I did use my hand. My hand jus' happened t'be holdin' a belt!"*

(They all collapse with slightly buzzed laughter…)

For years, I couldn't even recall that moment 'cause it literally scared me straight. I mean, that's probably why I blocked it out.

SAM: Yeah, I bet. / MIKE: That's fuckin'…

ERNIE: But I'll tell ya', when she died,…I was around 32 or thereabouts, I remember speakin' at her funeral n'I brought up that story, n'when I tell you that I laughed so fuckin' hard, I almost capsized over the casket. People looked at me like I was fuckin' bat-shit crazy but, I dunno', it jus' all came out that way.

MIKE: Why d'ya think?

ERNIE: I guess 'cause, in the end, I realized that them rhinestone welts in my ass were the difference in me takin' the other path I was headin' down. n'believe you me,…it wasn't the fuckin' *garden* path. *(He chuckles, swigs…)*

SAM: That's somethin', man.

MIKE: Hey, so now you're workin' *on* gardens insteada' bein' *under* 'em.

ERNIE: Hey, good one, Mike. See, he's learnin', Sam. There's poetry in everythin'!

MIKE: There y'go.

ERNIE: *(Takes a last swig…)* Well, I'm gonna' call it a night myself. You guys gonna' hang?

MIKE: Yeah, I'll stay. Sam, y'wana' do another around?

SAM: Yeah, why not.

   (ERNIE puts a bill on the table…)

ERNIE: Round's on me, okay? Enjoy, guys.

MIKE: Thanks, Ern… / SAM: Thanks, man…

ERNIE: See ya' Monday.

MIKE: See ya', Ern. / SAM: Yeah, be good, Ernie.

   (ERNIE exits off…)

MIKE: Good guy, right?

SAM: Ern? Yeah, he's a hoot.

MIKE: First guy I worked under that wasn't an asshole.

SAM: Yeah?

MIKE: Oh, yeah. Every place I was at before - retail, office; all fuckin' douchebags.

SAM: What'd you do in an office?

MIKE: Ah, it was a fluke thing my brother got me when I finished high school. Needed somethin', so I was makin' cold calls for this financial advisor. Like outbound callin' t'companies'n schools, and I was s'pposed to book appointments for 'im to come'n speak. Fuckin' nightmare.

SAM: Sounds it.

MIKE: Y'don't know the half, man. It was fuckin' shady too, n'I was buildin' this guy up like he was the second comin' a' financial Christ.

SAM: No?

MIKE: Oh, fuck no. He was some accountant who lost his license n'made a coupla' How-to videos on YouTube, which my mother coulda' made if she knew how to turn on a fuckin' computer. Anyway, he was always breathin' down my neck n'pushin' everyone to book these bullshit appointments, n'I couldn't book shit, so I couldn't make any commission. So I was only makin' the base pay which was less than a bartender makes, n' at least they get tips. n'I had to fuckin' shake this guy down jus' for that. Fuckin' asshole, man. Then one day he tried to dress me down about my production n'I like totally went off on 'im. I'd had it, man.

SAM: What'd y'do?

MIKE: I called 'im a prick n'threatened to throw him out the fuckin' window.

SAM: No shit.

MIKE: Oh, yeah. I was done.

SAM: So I guess that was that, huh?

MIKE: Yeah, that's usually that when you threaten to kill your boss.

>   *(They both laugh…)*

Anyway, those were the kinda' experiences I was havin' until I got into landscapin'. Workin' outside'n all. Still could be workin' for a prick, but I lucked out with Ern, y'know?

SAM: Good guy.

MIKE: Yeah, man.

SAM: Seems like he's got your back.

MIKE: Yeah, totally. *(Takes a swig, slight pause.)* Funny, where I'm from, you never see black dudes, y'know?

SAM: Yeah, I know where you're from.

MIKE: My mother to this day watches the news, sees blacks rioting n'gettin' busted n'shit, n'she thinks that's all of 'em. *"They're all criminals"*, she says. That's probably a lot a' the country, y'know? They don't know. They see shit with these scumbags, n'that's what some of 'em are, y'know? But they think that's all of 'em 'cause they don't know any. Then they see one in person, n'their hand goes for their pockets, or they roll their windows like they're on safari, or whatever. My brothers, guys I hang out with in my 'hood – they're fuckin' all like that. I used t'be that way too, man.

SAM: n'now you're reformed?

MIKE: Well, y'know, I'm not sayin' I'm holier than... Jus' everyone's different, is what I'm sayin'. Everyone can fall on one side or the other. Good or bad. I know that now. I didn't before, 'cause I didn't go far enough from the tree, y'know? You know, the apple doesn't... You know what I mean.

SAM: Yeah, the apple thing. I know. *(Swigs.)*

    (A moment, as they drink...)

MIKE: Anyway... *(Swigs.)* So y'miss bein' a cop?

SAM: *(A beat, swigs.)* No.

MIKE: *(Slight pause.)* Man, you're tight-lipped about it, shit.

SAM: Mike, c'mon, like I said the other day, I jus' don't like to talk about it, y'know...?

MIKE: Okay. I guess I jus' don't understand why you're downplayin' it. I got a lot a' respect for cops, Sam.

SAM: Yeah, I'm sure...

MIKE: Hell, I told ya' I wanted t'be one at one point.

SAM: It's jus' personal, that's all. Like you got things that you probably don't wana' talk about.

MIKE: Nah, I'll pretty much talk about anything.

SAM: Well, that's where we're different, okay? I put in a lota' years, had some experiences, n'now I kinda' wana' move on from it. That's all.

MIKE: Sure. Sorry, man.

SAM: No, look, it's cool. n'I appreciate ya' not sayin' anything to the guys about it.

MIKE: C'mon, you said not to mention it, n'I'm keepin' my word.

SAM: Thanks, man. You're a good guy. Y'remind me a lot a' some guys I used t'know, n'I feel like I can trust you so, y'know, I appreciate it, okay?

MIKE: Sure, man.

SAM: I mean, at this point in my life, you'd be surprised what that…y'know…

MIKE: *(A beat.)* What?

SAM: Jus'… Thanks, Mike.

MIKE: Hey, no worries, Sam. Look, you're good people. You know your shit n'you're a good fit. Everyone likes ya'.

    (A moment, as they swig.)

Can I jus' ask ya', though?

SAM: *(With a barely indulgent grin.)* Ask me what?

MIKE: Is 'at how you got the limp?

SAM: *(Slight pause.)* Yeah.

MIKE: Shit.

SAM: Yep.

MIKE: What happened?

SAM: *(Swigs..., slight pause.)* Took one in the thigh during a robbery attempt. Not far from here, actually.

MIKE: Fuckin' shit. Was 'at when you left?

SAM: No. Was on disability for a few months, came back.

MIKE: No kiddin'.

SAM: Yeah. Gave me a Purple Heart, put me on desk duty'n then went back t'workin' a beat shortly after.

MIKE: Purple fuckin' heart, man...?!

SAM: *(Over "heart...")* Mike,...

MIKE: Sam, I don't know why you wouldn't want the guys t'know this, man...

SAM: 'Cause people feel differently about cops. That's why.

MIKE: Yeah, but...

SAM: Look, you'n me are white guys from Brooklyn. That's a little different than what some a' the other guys here may think.

MIKE: Yeah, but that don't mean they hate cops...

SAM: You'd be surprised.

MIKE: Nah, I think…

SAM: Mike, y'don't know…

MIKE: Sam, y'served the city. You protected people. That includes these guys. They get it.

SAM: Mike, listen t'me, I was a cop for 10 years, okay? We were fuckin' despised.

MIKE: By everybody?

SAM: By a lota' minorities, n'do-gooder caucasians, n'the city government, even Giuliani didn't always have our backs, let alone the guy they got now who jus' can't wait to cut the ribbon on this park, okay? There's perception n'there's reality. n'the only way t'know the reality of a cop's life is t'be a cop. n'I was, okay? I put in 10 years, Mike, risked my life every fuckin' day, got shot, got shot *at*, didn't get a lot a' respect when I was there n'left with shit. That's why I don't talk about it. *(…swigs…)*

MIKE: *(Slight pause.)* How'd y'leave with shit?

SAM: Whata' y'mean?

MIKE: You were there 10 years. You don't get some kinda' pension…?

SAM: *(Over "pension…")* No, I don't.

MIKE: Aren't you supposed to…?

SAM: They let me go, Mike.

MIKE: *(Slight pause.)* They let you go? You got a purple fuckin' heart…

SAM: *(Over "heart…")* Mike,… *(Slight pause.)* I went to prison.
   (Lights)

   End of Act 1

ACT TWO

Scene 1

Morning, MIKE and ERNIE with coffees in hand.
One month later.

MIKE: I fuckin' told you, right?

ERNIE: Yeah, alright…

MIKE: I fuckin' told you…

ERNIE: If they knew their ass from their balls…

MIKE: *(Over "balls…")* What'd I tell ya'?

ERNIE: Alright, alright…

MIKE: How fuckin' cool is 'at?

ERNIE: Yeah, yeah…

MIKE: Right?

ERNIE: Yeah.

MIKE: Lemme see it again.

ERNIE: What? C'mon, Mike…

MIKE: I'm serious.

ERNIE: I jus' showed it to ya'…

MIKE: I wana' see it again, with the letterhead'n all.

ERNIE: *(A beat, before he pulls letter out of back pocket...)* It is pretty cool, right?

MIKE: Fuck yeah, it is.

ERNIE: *(Hands him letter...)* Alright, here.

MIKE: Want me t'read it aloud?

ERNIE: Get the fuck outa' here...

MIKE: *(Over "here...")* C'mon...

ERNIE: Nah...

MIKE: C'mon...

ERNIE: Mike...

MIKE: I'm gonna' fuckin' read it.

ERNIE: Yeah, what the hell.

(...as JOSE enters with backpack and coffee.)

MIKE: Hah! Alright. "Dear Mr. Bennett..."

JOSE: Ern, I need t'talk to ya' about...

MIKE: *(Over "talk to ya'...")* Jose, listen t'this, okay?

JOSE: What?

MIKE: Jus' fuckin' listen.

ERNIE: Jesus Christ...

MIKE: "Dear Mr. Bennett – We are pleased to inform you that your poem – *Dedication* – has been approved by our selection committee and we wish to grant you the opportunity of its reci – reci…" Dude, what the fuck?

ERNIE: Recitation.

MIKE: "…of its recitation at the opening for the heretofore named Harmony Park this fall."

JOSE: What's 'is?

ERNIE: Don't worry about it.

MIKE: Ern's gonna' read his poem at the opening a' the park.

JOSE: What park?

MIKE: Whata' y'mean 'what park'? *This* park.

JOSE: Yeah?

ERNIE: Yeah.

JOSE: Your poem?

ERNIE: Yeah.

MIKE: Cool, huh?

JOSE: Yeah, man. Felicitaciones.

ERNIE: Yeah, grassy-ass.

JOSE: Look, man, is Sam around?

ERNIE: No, he's off.

JOSE: He comin' back?

ERNIE: Not today. He'll be back tomorrow. What's up?

JOSE: I need to talk to ya' about somethin'.

ERNIE: About what?

JOSE: I think I should jus' tell you for now.

ERNIE: Why?

JOSE: Whata' y'mean why? You're the foreman.

ERNIE: I know what I am. You can't jus' tell me?

JOSE: Yeah, I can jus' tell *you*, okay?

MIKE: It's cool. I should start on the paths anyway.

(...MIKE gives letter back to ERNIE...)

JOSE: Thanks, Mike.

MIKE: No prob.

(MIKE tosses coffee in the nearby can and heads off...)

ERNIE: What's up?

JOSE: Where'd he go?

ERNIE: Where'd who go?

JOSE: Sam.

ERNIE: I jus' told you, he needed the day off. He's signin' divorce papers.

JOSE: He's gettin' divorced?

ERNIE: Yeah, he is. Look, y'got somethin' to tell me or what?

JOSE: Yeah, alright. Look, y'know I been sayin' how I thought Sam looked familiar, right?

ERNIE: Yeah.

JOSE: I thought we met or somethin', but I wasn't sure…

ERNIE: *(Over "I wasn't sure…")* Got it, continue.

JOSE: Well, last night Isabel'n I had a fight. I slept on the couch, couldn't sleep causa' the fuckin' bar, so I started fuckin' around on the computer, googlin' shit…

ERNIE: This is one boring-ass story, Jose, if you're…

JOSE: *(Over "…if you're…")* Alright, alright, hold on. Then I decided to enter Sam's name.

ERNIE: Yeah?

JOSE: Turns out we never met, but now I know why he looked familiar t'me.

ERNIE: Why?

JOSE: D'you know he was a cop?

ERNIE: *(A beat.)* Sam was a cop?

JOSE: Y'didn't know?

ERNIE: I didn't hire 'im, Jose. How'm I gonna' know unless he brought it up?

JOSE: So he hasn't brought it up.

ERNIE: No. Alright, so he was a cop. What else?

JOSE: You ever hear about the case with that guy, black dude, he was arrested 'cause these cops thought he robbed a bodega n'they ended up beatin' this guy so bad, he had like a ruptured spleen'n shit?

ERNIE: That sounds like every other case I read about these days.

JOSE: It was like 10 years ago. Luello Harris? He died in the hospital a week later.

ERNIE: Yeah, alright, vaguely.

JOSE: Y'remember?

ERNIE: Yeah.

JOSE: I knew a guy who knew Luello.

ERNIE: Alright, so what does Sam have t'do with this?

JOSE: What does he have t'do with it? He was one a' the cops that beat the fuck outa' this guy, man. His name came up in these articles I found. He and three other cops were responsible for killin' 'im, n'it turns out he was the wrong guy anyway.

ERNIE: *(Slight pause.)* You serious?

JOSE: *(Pulls out I-Phone…)* Yeah, man. His photo's there plain as day.

> *(Gives it to Ern to view…)*

He went t'fuckin' prison, man. Served two years. The guy who was the ringleader is still servin'. I think he's a transsexual now or some shit. Hey, he's servin' 30 – may as well be, right?

> *(ERNIE continues to view the image on JOSE's phone…)*

Yeah, they kicked Sam off the force, man. Had his Purple Heart taken away. Fuckin' blackballed.

> *(A moment, as JOSE looks at ERNIE still looking at phone…)*

Whata' y'think, Ern?

ERNIE: I dunno'.

JOSE: Thass fuckin' crazy, right?

ERNIE: Yeah, it is.

JOSE: Right on our own crew. Over a month now. Who knew?

ERNIE: I sure didn't.

JOSE: Me neither, man. But I couldn't get it outa' my head that I recognized him from somethin', y'know? It was drivin' me nuts.

(ERNIE remains stunned...)

Whata' y'think, Ern?

ERNIE: Jose, I don't know, okay? Can y'stop askin' me that? Jus' lemme sit with this. Fuck, we gotta' damn job t'do, y'know?

JOSE: I know.

(They remain a moment...)

You upset I told ya'?

ERNIE: Jose, please...

JOSE: No, I mean, I don't want y'thinkin' I'm rattin' the guy out. I mean, we've had ex-cons work with us before, but this jus' seemed like somethin'...

ERNIE: *(Over "somethin'...")* Don't worry about it.

JOSE: I mean, everyone's got shit from their past, but this is some serious...

ERNIE: Jose, I'm not upset at ya', okay? We had t'know this.

JOSE: We did, right?

ERNIE: Yeah, we did.

(A moment, as ERNIE continues to ponder...)

JOSE: So...whata' y'gonna do?

ERNIE: I dunno' jus' yet.

JOSE: I mean, they musta' known when they hired 'im, right?

ERNIE: Yeah.

JOSE: Right?

ERNIE: He said he knew someone.

JOSE: Whata' y'mean?

ERNIE: He told me'n Mike he got a reference from someone who knew someone in the front office, so obviously they musta' known.

JOSE: They do background checks anyway.

ERNIE: Yeah.

JOSE: *(Slight pause.)* So…what's 'at mean?

ERNIE: You tell anyone on the crew?

JOSE: Not yet.

ERNIE: Well, don't. Jus' do your job'n everyone else can focus on theirs.

JOSE: n'what?

ERNIE: What? I dunno' what, Jose. We gotta' job t'do. That's all I know.

(They remain a moment…)

JOSE: Y'don't think Mike knows?

ERNIE: Mike? No.

JOSE: I'm sayin' maybe Sam told 'im.

ERNIE: Why would Sam tell 'im?

JOSE: You know. They talk, kinda' like you'n Mike. Maybe shit slipped…

ERNIE: Nah.

JOSE: Coulda' come up.

ERNIE: Mike woulda' told me.

JOSE: *(Slight pause.)* Yeah, I guess.

ERNIE: Let's get started, okay? We're already short today, we don't need t'slack too.

JOSE: Alright.

ERNIE: I'll be there in a minute. Jus' make sure everyone's on the same page, okay?

JOSE: Yeah.

ERNIE: Thanks.

JOSE: You okay?

ERNIE: Fine.

JOSE: You sure?

ERNIE: Yeah, don't worry.

JOSE: *(Slight pause.)* Fucked up, right?

(JOSE looks at ERNIE before exiting off. ERNIE remains, unusually pensive…)

(Lights)

Scene 2

The next morning. As the lights come up, we hear morning sparrow chirps, distant clanging metal from rakes, hoes, etc. MIKE is pouring rocks into a path framed by 2x4s, which is being spread out with a hoe by SAM…

SAM: Yeah, it was strange, y'know?

MIKE: I bet.

SAM: With someone for almost 20 years, n'alluvasudden it comes down to a signature. Jus' sittin' there, starin' at this pieca' paper, n'it's like the whole relationship rushes in fronta' ya', y'know? Things I forgot about; where we met, what she wore, the stupid line I had, our wedding, the shoe leather veal at the reception, band playin' Billy Joel'n shit…

MIKE: Yeah, man.

SAM: Her givin' birth to our kids, their communion, confirmation… Jesus, a snap of a fuckin' finger, man.

MIKE: Yeah…

SAM: Snap of a fuckin' finger, from the shitty pub we met at to this lawyer's office, with this pieca' paper. Sign y'name, done.

MIKE: *(Slight pause.)* Sorry, dude.

SAM: Hey, whata' y'gonna' do.

(As SAM continues to spread stones…)

MIKE: You guys at least able to talk'n stuff?

SAM: Nah, it's all custody shit now. That's pretty much where we're at. Where, when… It's like we existed long enough for them to walk, n'now we basically gotta' parent across a fuckin' tightrope. Her on one side, me on the other – we gotta' jus' make sure they don't fall off, while they're goin' back'n forth like a fuckin' yo-yo. Jus' gotta' hope that when they're 18, she hasn't filled their heads with so much shit that they don't wana' see me anymore.

MIKE: Y'think she would?

SAM: Why not? She's gettin' money from me. She's gettin' more time than I am. She can say she invented the fuckin' light-bulb n'all I did was take too long in the bathroom, f'Godsakes…

MIKE: Maybe not, y'know? Who knows.

SAM: I dunno', Mike…

(ERNIE comes on…)

ERNIE: How we lookin'?

MIKE: Good, Ern.

SAM: Yeah, jus' smoothin' it out.

ERNIE: Well, not doin' too good, from where I'm at.

SAM: Whata' y'mean?

ERNIE: Y'gotta' slope goin' there. Y'don't see that? Put a straight ruler across that.

SAM: Alright, well, I wasn't done, Ern.

ERNIE: *(Over "I wasn't done...")* We off by an inch, that's more work for us later on. You lay that Gravel-Lok down on a slope, the inspectors'll be all over that. We're on enough of a time crunch as it is.

SAM: Alright, well, I'll triple check before we lay down anything.

MIKE: It's on me too, Ern. I gotta' have eyes too...

ERNIE: Mike, Sam's got enough experience. That's why he's here.

SAM: I jus' said I'll be on it, Ern, okay?

ERNIE: *(A beat, as he looks intently at Sam...)* Yeah.

> *(A moment, as ERNIE and SAM look at each other, MIKE at the two of them...)*

SAM: Everything else okay, Ern?

ERNIE: *(Slight pause.)* Yeah, fine.

> *(ERNIE keeps his eyes on SAM, before slowly going off...)*

SAM: What the hell, man?

MIKE: I dunno'.

SAM: He's been ridin' me all mornin'.

MIKE: He'll be okay. C'mon.

(*SAM continues to look off...*)

Sam, c'mon. Don't sweat it. He's jus' stressin' a little, that's all. It's everybody, man. Not jus' you.

SAM: Y'think so?

MIKE: Yeah.

SAM: Seems like it's jus' me, Mike.

MIKE: It's not.

SAM: I don't see him ridin' anyone else like this.

MIKE: Trust me, man. Don't take it personally, okay? The fuckin' parks commissioner is breathin' down our necks 'cause a' the fuckin' election year bullshit'n all. It's cool, man. C'mon.

(*SAM continues to look off, before going back to smoothing gravel...*)

(*A moment.*)

MIKE: So they finally gotta' name for this place, huh?

SAM: (*Distracted...*) Yeah.

MIKE: Harmony Park. It'll probably fall on deaf ears here. I give it 2 weeks before some asshole spray-paints D-I-S in fronta' Harmony. They'll probably call us back in a month to resod the grass after someone tries to bury their cat in it, right?

(MIKE laughs, attempting to get a reaction from SAM...)

SAM: Yeah.

MIKE: You weren't here yesterday - we found fuckin' syringes on the ground. Y'believe that?

SAM: No.

MIKE: They're hoppin' over the barrier jus' to shoot up. No one mentioned it to ya'?

SAM: No.

MIKE: Unbefuckinlievable, huh?

SAM: Yeah.

MIKE: Can y'imagine what this place is gonna' turn into when we're done? Here we're plantin' all these beautiful flowers, fuckin' lilacs, daffodils, African violets... They'll probably rip 'em right outa' the ground n'try'n sell 'em for an 8 ball or some shit.

SAM: Yeah.

MIKE: I mean, this is gonna' be a nice fuckin' park, y'know? Probably the nicest one I worked on. Fountain, fresh grass, handball court on the other side. All this work, man...

SAM: *(Stops hoeing...)* This look even t'you?

MIKE: *(A beat.)* Yeah, it's even.

SAM: Right?

MIKE: Yeah.

SAM: Should we get the straight ruler on it?

MIKE: No, man. It's even.

SAM: So if he busts my chops again, I got you t'back me up, right?

MIKE: It's even, Sam. What's up?

SAM: You know what's up. He's up to somethin'.

MIKE: Who?

SAM: Ernie.

MIKE: What?

SAM: You didn't tell 'im anything?

MIKE: About…?

SAM: Yeah.

MIKE: No, man.

SAM: Y'sure?

MIKE: Yeah, man. I didn't tell anybody.

SAM: I jus' wana' do my job'n not be set up.

MIKE: No one's settin' you up, Sam…

SAM: How d'you know?

MIKE: I know.

SAM: No, y'don't.

MIKE: I don't but I do, okay? No one here would pull that...

SAM: You're friends with 'im, Mike.

MIKE: That don't matter...

SAM: It does, n'you know it.

MIKE: Sam,...

SAM: You're not lookin' at the situation right, Mike. I didn't hide anything from HR, okay? Someone coulda' contacted them or found out shit on me. You know exactly what I'm talkin' about.

MIKE: C'mon, Sam...

SAM: They coulda' read some shit...

MIKE: Sam, it's cool, okay...?

SAM: Y'know, this ain't exactly a high-end gig for me, okay? But I didn't have a fuckin' choice.

MIKE: Yeah, I get it...

SAM: *(Over "get it...")* I need a Goddamn job.

MIKE: Yeah, I hear ya', man. Look, jus' cool down......

SAM: *(Over "Look, jus...")* I gotta' pay alimony, I gotta' pay child support, not t'mention my own rent'n n bills. I don't need somebody fuckin' sabotaging me!

(As ERNIE comes on...)

MIKE: Dude, cool down, okay...?

ERNIE: What's goin' on?

MIKE: It's cool, Ern... / SAM: Everything's fuckin' fine, Ern!

MIKE: Dude, look... Ern, lemme talk to ya'...

ERNIE: *(Over "Ern, lemme talk...")* What'd you say?

MIKE: Ern, it's cool... / SAM: You heard what I said.

MIKE: Sam, cool down, okay?!

ERNIE: *(Over "okay...")* You gotta' problem with somethin', Sam?

(A moment, as SAM and ERNIE look at each other...)

Do ya'?

SAM: Yeah, I *do* gotta' problem. I gotta' problem with some-one findin' fault with nothin', okay?

ERNIE: Whata' you mean nothin'?

SAM: You know what I mean.

ERNIE: You can't smooth out gravel, that's a fault worth findin'.

SAM: I know how to smooth out gravel, Ernie. I was doin' more extensive jobs than this before I knew you.

ERNIE: You can't make a mistake?

SAM: Everyone makes mistakes, but that's not what this is about.

ERNIE: This is about everyone workin' together n'gettin' things done right so they don't gotta' be done again.

SAM: I'm doin' it right.

ERNIE: What I saw you doin' was not right, okay? n'it's my job to make sure it gets done right.

SAM: *(Over "it gets done right...")* Oh, gimme a break, Ern. Really.

ERNIE: Give you a break?

SAM: You think layin' down a gravel path is rocket science?

MIKE: Whoa, Sam, c'mon now...

ERNIE: No one's askin' you t'do rocket science, Sam. They're askin' you to lay down gravel.

SAM: n'I'm doin' it.

ERNIE: And you made a mistake.

SAM: I didn't make a mistake. I wasn't done!

MIKE: Sam, calm down, okay? Ern, lemme jus'...

SAM: *(Over "Ern, lemme, jus…")* No, Mike, enougha' this bull-shit. I don't need to have a foreman with delusions a' grandeur tellin' me how to lay down a fuckin' path!

ERNIE: *(Over "tellin' me how to…")* Delusions a' fuckin' gran-deur…?

SAM: I been landscapin' privately for 6 years, makin' a lot more money than I'm makin' here. I oversaw 25 guys, okay? Trained 'em all – excavation, gardening, mulching, concrete, stone-work…

ERNIE :   /   MIKE:
(Over "concrete, stonework…")   Sam, calm down, okay…?!
I don't need t'hear your damn resume…

> *(As MIKE attempts to gently push SAM away from ER-NIE…)*

SAM: No, Mike, I'm not playin' this shit.

ERNIE: I ain't playin' shit either. Go home for the day.

SAM: n'what, you think I'm gonna' come back tomorrow n'deal with your shit?

ERNIE: I didn't say you're comin' back tomorrow. I said you can go home today.

SAM: Yeah, n'guess what, I'll bring this up with HR and maybe *you* won't be here tomorrow.

ERNIE: n'how d'you propose to do that?

SAM: How? This is a violation a' my rights, okay?

ERNIE: You gonna' tell me about violatin' rights…?

SAM: *(Over "violatin' rights…")* You're pullin' shit n'I know why.

ERNIE: I ain't violatin' shit. This is my job.

SAM: No, this ain't your job.

ERNIE: Don't tell me what my job is! You gonna' give me my Goddamn job description….?!!!

SAM: *(Over "Goddamn job description…")* Harrassing employees is not parta' your…!!!

MIKE	/	ERNIE:
(Over "not parta' your…") Guys, Guys, Guys….!!!		You landscaped for some Long Island company for a half dozen years n'you think that gives you the right to talk about your rights bein' violated?!!! What'd you do before those 6 years, huh, Sam?!!!

SAM: *(Over "6 years…")* Yeah, that's right, keep yappin', Ern… Keep yappin', keep yappin', keep yappin'…

ERNIE: *(Over "keep yappin', Ern…")* You wana' talk about violating rights? Huh? You wana' talk about violatin' rights?

(ERNIE throws a nearby rake to the ground…)

TALK TO LUELLO HARRIS, MOTHERFUCKER!!!

(A moment, as ERNIE and SAM stare at each other, as if on the verge of violence… MIKE can only observe cautiously.)

SAM: See? *(Slight pause, to Mike.)* Looka' that.

ERNIE: Look at what?

(A moment.)

SAM: Fuckin' gravel path.

(A moment.)

ERNIE: I think you better go, Sam.

SAM: Oh, you do.

ERNIE: Yeah, I do.

(A moment of this continued stillness, as SAM holds hoe...)

SAM: Y'know, when I was a cop, I learned a very important thing, Ern. Y'want the truth, y'ask the questions. That's how y'get the right answers. *(A beat.)* Coulda' jus' asked me, Ern. *(A beat.)* All y'had t'do.

(SAM slams the hoe to the ground, looks at MIKE then ERNIE, before storming off...)

(ERNIE continues to look off intensely. MIKE looks off as well, before coming back to ERNIE...)

MIKE: You okay?

(A moment...)

Ern...?

ERNIE: You knew?

MIKE: *(Slight pause.)* That he was a cop? Yeah…

ERNIE: What he did.

MIKE: *(Slight pause.)* Yeah, but…

ERNIE: You did.

MIKE: Ern, listen…

ERNIE: He told you?

MIKE: It was over some drinks, n'he…

ERNIE: When?

MIKE: Ern, c'mon…

ERNIE: Jus' askin' a question. When, Mike?

MIKE: Like a month ago.

ERNIE: *(A beat.)* A month you've known this?

MIKE: Yeah.

ERNIE: n'it didn't cross your mind to tell me this?

MIKE: It did.

ERNIE: But y'didn't.

MIKE: Ern, he asked me not to, okay?

ERNIE: Not to tell me.

MIKE: Not to tell anybody.

ERNIE: So he asked you n'that was enough.

MIKE: Ern, look, it's not like he lied to anyone. He didn't lie on his interviews. He told 'em everything. They knew.

ERNIE: n'you knew.

MIKE: Ern, look, everybody likes 'im. No one's had a beef with 'im...

ERNIE: They didn't know.

MIKE: Right, n'he didn't want 'em to.

ERNIE: Who gives a shit what he wanted, Mike?! You shoulda' told me!

MIKE: *(Slight pause.)* Why, Ern?

ERNIE: What the hell you mean why?

MIKE: So you can almost come to blows a month ago insteada' today?

ERNIE: Hey, it's one month I coulda' gone without thinkin' he was someone he wasn't.

MIKE: Ern, he's not on the fuckin' lam, okay? He did the time, he's out, n'that's it...

ERNIE: That's it? You think that's it? That ain't *nearly* fuckin' it. Motherfucker gets a slap on the wrist for bein' a corrupt cop so he can jus' work wherever he wants now?

MIKE: He can't work wherever he wants. He needed this job, Ern...

ERNIE: A lota' guys need jobs, Mike, n'I'd rather have one who hasn't jammed a nightstick up some guy's ass!

MIKE: Ern, he didn't even do the shit they said!

ERNIE: How d'you know?

MIKE: 'cause he told me.

ERNIE: n'you believe 'im?

MIKE: Yeah, I believe 'im. Why should I believe anyone else who wasn't even there, Ern? He was there.

ERNIE: n'you don't think for a second he's fulla' shit?

MIKE: No, he's...

ERNIE: You think you really know this guy?

MIKE: Ern, listen t'me. He told me he was in the wrong place at the wrong time n'he got roped into shit...

ERNIE: *(Over "roped into shit...")* Are you kiddin' me...?

MIKE: Ern, listen t'me, okay? There were like 4 cops involved, right? Only one did mosta' the shit. Yeah, they all got carried away, but Sam mainly stood by. He lied t'cover the other guys. That's the code, y'know? Y'don't rat. He didn't, n'he went down with the ship. He got 2 years 'cause he lied, Ern, not 'causa' the guy gettin' killed.

ERNIE: Even if I believed that shit, there's somethin' missin' in a man who would stand by n'let shit like that happen…

MIKE: *(Over "like that happen…")* I'm not sayin' he wasn't wrong…

ERNIE: No, Mike, I'm sayin' that there's somethin' seriously wrong with him n'I can't work with it n'I ain't *gonna'* work with it, y'hear me?

MIKE: *(A beat.)* Fine, it's your call, Ern.

ERNIE: No, it ain't my call. I gotta' wait t'hear back from HR. They're the ones who gotta' say.

MIKE: You already contacted 'em?

ERNIE: Damn straight.

MIKE: Ern, c'mon…

ERNIE: That's what the hell they're there for, Mike. If I gotta' concern about somethin' that conflicts with my job, they're gonna' hear about it.

MIKE: *(Slight pause.)* Look, Ern, you can feel how you want to about it but, y'know, think about it.

ERNIE: Think about what?

MIKE: This coulda' been a pregnant lady, an ol' man, a kid. It was a 220 lb, 6'4" dude with a record, okay?

ERNIE: A *black* dude.

MIKE: A big fuckin' dude.

ERNIE: Yeah, right…

MIKE: With a record.

ERNIE: A record for what?! Illegal fireworks?!

MIKE: That's a fuckin' crime!

ERNIE: So you kill a black man over fireworks but a bad white cop gets t'work here with me?

MIKE: Ern, look…

ERNIE: n'probably gets offered a foreman job in half the time it took me, t'boot?!!! Who the hella' you to defend that motherfucker t'me, Mike!!!

    (JOSE appears…)

No matter how you wana' slice'n dice it, they were 4 on 1. They weren't in danger. They took an unarmed, innocent man, in his own home with his wife'n kid in the next room, n'tortured that motherfucker 'til he was dead. Sam was there. Sam did somethin'. I don't care what the fuck you wana' believe jus' 'cause he told it to ya'. You know that motherfucker for jus' over a month n'you're defendin' him like he's your long lost goomba brotha'.

MIKE: Ern, you need to chill the fuck out…

ERNIE: *(Over "Chill the fuck out…")* You have the balls to question why I would feel like this.

MIKE: I'm not takin' sides, Ern…

ERNIE: I've lived twice your life n'three lifetimes, n'you haven't even moved outa' your mother's house, n'you're gonna' try'n school me?!

MIKE: *(Over "try'n school me…?")* Ern, listen t'me…

ERNIE: You don't know your ass from the holes you been diggin', my friend. You hear me? You don't know jack shit!

MIKE: *(Slight pause.)* Ern, look, you're pissed'n shit, so why don't you vent to the air, okay…?

(…as MIKE starts off…)

ERNIE: Oh, you gonna' give me permission?

MIKE: What?

ERNIE: I got your ok to bitch to the birds, Mike?!

MIKE: Look, you wana' hate Sam, hate 'im. Okay? I didn't do shit. I wasn't there. He told me, I kept my word, that don't put me at the fuckin' scene, okay?

ERNIE: I ain't sayin' you were there.

MIKE: Then whata' you sayin'?

ERNIE: I'm sayin' you shoulda' told me.

MIKE: 'cause you're my boss? 'cause you're black? Why, Ern?

ERNIE: *(Over "Why, Ern?")* 'cause I thought I was your fuckin' friend n'hidin' somethin' like this makes me wonder if you're jus' like him!

(A still moment.)

MIKE: Why you gotta' go there, Ern?

ERNIE: 'Cause there's no other place for me t'be at the moment, Mike.

MIKE: Unbefuckinlievable…

ERNIE: You wana' justify what happened by sayin' that guy had it comin', so you'd rather have the back a' some corrupt asshole over someone who treated you like a damn son…

MIKE: Don't pull this shit, Ern. Okay?

ERNIE: *(Over "Okay?")* I ain't pullin' shit, Mike…

MIKE: Don't fuckin' lump me with every white guy who doesn't hate all cops n'put a fuckin' white sheet in my closet. That's fuckin' bullshit.

ERNIE: *(Over "That's fuckin' bullshit…")* Don't you tell me what I'm doin'…

MIKE: What, I'm s'pposed t'jus' say every black dude is a saint, like every pussy fuckin' democrat you want me t'vote for?

(…as JOSE moves in closer…)

ERNIE: You better back off… /   JOSE: Guys, c'mon, we got work t'do, right…?

MIKE: *(Over "we got work t'do…")* Who were those 4 kids who raped those girls here, Ern?

ERNIE: We're done, Mike…

MIKE: Y'think they were fuckin' Irish?

ERNIE: Mike,…

MIKE: 4 Black dudes, Ern!!!

JOSE: Mike, c'mon, man, let's…

MIKE: *(Over "c'mon, let's…")* n'y'know what? We finish this park, the same shit'll happen again. Mark my fuckin' words. That ain't racist, Ern! That's fuckin' reality.

ERNIE: *(Over "fuckin' reality…")* Mike, we're done…

MIKE: Yeah, go ahead n'read your little poem, Ern…

ERNIE: *(Over "your little poem…")* Get outa' my sight…

MIKE: Make yourself believe that this is gonna' mean shit when it's all over…!!!

ERNIE: ENOUGH!!!

> *(A still moment.)*

You better get outa' my sight right now.

> *(MIKE and ERNIE continue to gaze at each other, as JOSE observes them…)*

> *(A moment.)*

MIKE: n'I ain't your fuckin' son. Y'understand me?

> *(A moment, before MIKE goes off.)*

> *(ERNIE and JOSE remain.)*

JOSE*:* Ernie, what the fuck…

ERNIE: Jose, go back t'work n'make sure everyone else is…

> *(Ernie looks off, as if noticing workers looking on…)*

WHAT THE HELLA' YOU ALL LOOKIN' AT?! AIN'T

NOTHIN' T'SEE HERE, ALRIGHT?!!! EVERYTHING'S
FINE!!! Jose, you up my ass enough for my job, why don't
you do it now while I get my head together.

JOSE: You okay? Wana' coffee or somethin'…?

ERNIE: I'm fine.

JOSE: *(Slight pause.)* Jesucristo, I wish I didn't find out, man. I
really wish… Aye dio…

> *(JOSE looks at ERNIE, gazing off, as if still decompress-*
> *ing from the events… JOSE starts off…)*

Okay, guys! Matinee's over!!! Vamos a volver al trabajo…!

> *(Once JOSE is off, ERNIE takes a moment, before sud-*
> *denly kicking the gravel into the air, and pushing over the*
> *nearby wheelbarrow. ERNIE pants heavily at this ac-*
> *tion,…as the lights fade….)*

> *(*In dim light, we see the park developing to indicate the*
> *passage of time. Some grass sod patches are laid, a path*
> *over the gravel lane, a fountain installed, some flowers,*
> *etc. This should be done with music, with the light dim*
> *enough to render the workers indistinguishable from one*
> *another.)*

Scene 3

A pub in the city. Ambient sounds of clinking glasses and inaudi-
ble conversations, which fade into SAM at bar stool, beer in hand,
as if watching a distant TV screen. After a moment, MIKE enters.
It is about 2 months later…

SAM: Hey, man.

MIKE: Hey, what's up?

(As they shake…)

SAM*:* Good to see ya'. How's it goin'?

MIKE*:* Eh, y'know. s'been a while, huh?

SAM*:* Yeah, what, like 2 months?

MIKE: Yeah, I guess.

SAM: *(A chuckle…)* Since our last day at that fuckin' park.

MIKE: Yeah, man.

SAM: Wana' beer?

MIKE: Yeah, maybe in a bit.

SAM: Lemme get ya' somethin'.

MIKE: I'm okay f'now, man. Thanks. Maybe later.

SAM: Alright. So how's it goin'?

MIKE: Eh, y'know. Same shit. Lookin' for work.

SAM: I hear that.

MIKE: Lookin' at some commercial companies, but no one's hirin'. You?

SAM: Same.

MIKE: Sucks, right?

SAM: Yeah, man. Got a coupla' vibes out to some places, but who knows. The job market pretty much sucks no matter what you're lookin' for.

MIKE: You ain't kiddin'.

SAM: Better off livin' at home, like you, with how things are. Believe me, if I could, I would.

MIKE: If you had a different mother, I'd recommend it, but I'm tryin' t'get outa' there now.

SAM: Why?

MIKE: Jus', y'know, 'cause.

SAM: Y'got no job n'you're gonna' move?

MIKE: When I get somethin', I mean. Hopefully that's soon'n, if it is, I'll start lookin' for my own place. Maybe jus' a room-mate situation. I dunno'.

SAM: Well, look, I'll recommend ya', if I get in any doors any time soon, okay?

MIKE: Thanks, man.

SAM: Hey, you're a friend n'you know your shit. Why wouldn't I?

MIKE: Appreciate it.

SAM: Sure.

MIKE: Whata' y'doin' in the meantime?

SAM: Whata' y'think? Fuckin' unemployment.

MIKE: You can get it after only being with the Parks for like a month?

SAM: Nah, gettin' it through my previous job. I should be able t'get it through the Parks job, considerin' how they treated me, but the lawsuit should settle that.

MIKE: Yeah, so what's happenin' with 'at?

SAM: Gotta' good lawyer, recommended by my divorce lawyer. Suit's been filed for unlawful termination.

MIKE: Think y'can win?

SAM: Guy says they had no grounds t'let me go. I was doin' my job. You know that, right?

MIKE: Yeah, I know.

SAM: Can't let someone go 'cause the guy you work with don't like cops. I told 'em everything at my interview, they knew. I didn't withhold shit. They felt pressure 'cause a' fuckin' Ernie. That's why I was fired. He's got almost 20 years t'my month. Who'd y'think they'd side with?

MIKE: Yeah.

SAM: I should make out okay, though. The Parks commissioner don't want this publicized anymore than *I* do, so my lawyer said they can settle sooner.

MIKE: Cool, man.

SAM: n'there's certain things that'll help move it along too.

MIKE: Like what?

SAM: *(A smile, a swig...)* Like a witness.

MIKE: A witness t'what?

SAM: What *you* witnessed.

MIKE: *(An odd smile…)* What'd I witness?

SAM: Whata' y'talkin' about? You saw that Ernie was tryin' t'inch me out. He was tryin' t'get me to lose my shit.

MIKE: *(Slight pause.)* But he didn't fire ya'.

SAM: That's not the point. He's the one who put pressure on HR to fire me, Mike.

MIKE: Yeah, alright, but you're already suin' them. That's where the settlement'll come from if ya' win, right?

SAM: He's the reason the shit happened, Mike. He don't make a stink, I have my job still. You too, man. I get a testimony that says Ernie tried t'sabotage me, now they're pressured t'fire his ass.

MIKE: *(Slight pause, takes this in...)* Huh.

SAM: Y'understand now?

MIKE: *(Slight pause.)* Wait, so… Is 'at why you called me?

SAM: Nah, c'mon. I wanted t'see ya', man. I still consider ya' a friend, y'know. But I did wana' talk to ya' about it 'cause, y'know, it's better t'bring this kinda' stuff up in person.

MIKE: Uh-huh.

SAM: What, y'don't feel right about it?

MIKE: I dunno.

SAM: How can y'not?

MIKE: I guess I jus' didn't expect it. I mean, I'm not there anymore. I'm onto the next thing.

SAM: What thing?

MIKE: Whatever the hell, I dunno. I jus' didn't think…

SAM: I mean, it's not like you don't have an interest in this as well, right? You got fired.

MIKE: I didn't get fired.

SAM: I thought y'said you went off on Ernie n'you're not there anymore.

MIKE: Yeah, but I left. I never got fired. Ernie never even mentioned anything t'HR. I jus' left n'didn't come back.

SAM: Alright, well, look, maybe you didn' get fired, but you're not there because a' the shit Ernie pulled. You were forced into a situation where you had no choice but t'leave, right?

MIKE: Yeah, alright…

SAM: You knew I was right, n'you stuck t'your guns, man. n'you weren't gonna' let some guy get on his soapbox n'pull shit. n'you're a buddy for that, Mike. That took guts. You were there longer, you knew Ernie more, or y'*thought* y'did,…but y'saw he was crossin' a line. Saw 'im for who he is. See? You coulda' been a cop after all. *(He snickers, swigs…)*

(MIKE snickers along…)

You ain't no pussy. Salt a' the earth.

(SAM goes to toast, but MIKE has no drink, so he reluctantly fist bumps…)

Y'sure you don't wana' drink so we can do this right?

MIKE: No, I'm good. Thanks, Sam.

(SAM takes a swig, as they both look at distant screen for a moment...)

Y'think you were a good cop, Sam?

SAM: *(A beat.)* Yeah, I do. Why?

MIKE: *(A beat.)* Jus' askin'.

SAM: Why y'askin?

MIKE: Jus' curious.

SAM: Why?

MIKE: *(Slight pause.)* Y'don't got any regrets?

SAM: Whata' y'talkin' about, Mike?

MIKE: *(Slight pause.)* Did everything happen like y'said?

SAM: Did what happen?

MIKE: With that guy. Luello whatever?

SAM: *(A beat.)* Yeah, I told ya'.

MIKE: *(Slight pause.)* Y'jus' watched the door.

SAM: Mike, what is this? I told ya' all this.

MIKE: Alright.

SAM: You believe me, right?

MIKE: *(Slight pause, as he looks at screen...)* Yeah, I believe ya'.

SAM: Mike, I mean, am I askin' too much here? 'cause if I am, jus' tell me. I didn't think I was. Especially considerin' that if I get a nice settlement, I was plannin' t'start up my own company again n'wanted t'offer you a job, if y'wanted.

(MIKE looks at him…)

Yeah, no shit, man. You'd be a foreman right outa' the gate. I'm not the type that's gonna' take money n'sit on it. I gotta' work, man. May as well work for myself once I can afford it. Right? n'I'd be happy t'have ya' on board. You're a good landscaper.

MIKE: *(A beat.)* That's nice a' ya', Sam.

SAM: Fuck that. It ain't nice. It'd be my pleasure. You deserve it.

(A moment, as they look at the screen…)

MIKE: Do I deserve it *now*?

SAM: *(Smiles…)* Whata' y'mean? I don't got a pot t'piss in now, Mike…

MIKE: No, I mean,…do I get it if don't give my testimony?

SAM: *(Slight pause.)* What's the problem, Mike? Alluvasudden now you're lookin' out for that guy?

MIKE: No, I'm not…

SAM: Well, what the hell d'you care…?

MIKE: *(Over "d'you care…")* I jus' don't see why y'gotta' go after 'im.

SAM: Why? I ain't workin' now because a' him, okay? Because a' him, I have no way t'pay my alimony, pay child support, pay my bills on time... Y'think I can do that on unemployment, Mike?

MIKE: Sam, okay, but I mean, y'get the settlement n'that'll cover everything. What's all this other shit gonna' do...?

SAM: *(Over "this other shit gonna' do...")* Hold on, hold on, Mike, lemme ask ya' somethin', okay?

MIKE: What?

SAM: You remember you tellin' me about that guy you used t'work for who you hated. That financial guy who you threatened t'throw out the window?

MIKE: Yeah, what...?

SAM: Well, that was a death threat, wasn't it. n'you coulda' gotten yourself much worse than fired 'cause a' that.

MIKE: Sam, what does that...?

SAM: Mike, I'm sayin' that I'm takin' a very legal road here with Ernie. I can do this. This is not a threat a' violence. This is my right as an employee a' the Parks Department who had his rights taken away 'cause some uppity foreman thought he could play God with his crew. This motherfucker fucked up my life, n'he ain't gonna' get away with it if I have anything t'say about it. Now you don't wana' do so much as write a statement on a piece a' paper t'back me up? What can I tell ya', man? It'd be a big disappointment t'me, but hey,...it's up t'you.

> *(A moment, as SAM takes a hostile swig, looks at screen...)*

MIKE: Y'know,…my father was a real fuckin' asshole, man. Left us when I was a kid. I didn't get t'know 'em too well but I knew 'im enough t'know he hated jus' about everyone who didn't look like him. Didn't like 'em. Didn't trust 'em. My mother's like that, but she'd never do anything about it. She'd never say shit to anyone outside the house. But my father,…he'd say shit. He'd do shit.   Him'n my brothers n'me would chuck rocks at a black dude if we saw one in our neighborhood. I mean,… Then he split, n'I think I been kinda' lookin' for… Not him, but lookin' for somethin'. Not another father. Jus'… I dunno. I feel like I was gipped with him, y'know. Not 'cause he left. Because he was there at all. I mean, he was a scumbag, n'I hate his guts, n'if I ever saw 'im again, I don't know what I'd do, but it wouldn't be a fuckin' hug, I'll tell ya' that…

SAM: Mike, I don't know where the hell y'goin' with this, but…

MIKE: *(Over "goin' with this…")* I'm jus… I'm sayin' I never met a guy his age I even trusted until Ernie, n'it ended bad. n'I ain't sayin' he was right n'I ain't sayin' I was wrong, but…I'm kinda' bummed it ended like it did'n so I jus' kinda' wana' move on from it, Sam. That's all. I don't wana' come down on 'im anymore than I did. He pissed me off, don't get me wrong, but…enough's enough, y'know? Sorry.

SAM: Well, if that's enough f'you, Mike, what can I tell ya'. You're very lucky.

MIKE: How'm I lucky?

SAM: Y'don't got any concerns. No ex-wife, no kids. You can dust yourself off from all this as if it didn't happen, but I can't, okay?

MIKE: Sam, I ain't sayin' don't sue. Sue the Parks department, yeah, they got money t'burn, but jus' don't come down on Ernie. That's all I'm…

SAM: *(Over "That's all I'm...")* You don't fuckin' get it, Mike, do ya'?

MIKE: What's t'get?

SAM: One already fucked up my life one way 'cause he was black n'I wore a badge. I ain't gonna' let another off the hook. I ain't gettin' fucked over twice. Now you can either be loyal to a friend who's lookin' out for ya' or loyal t'some bullshit father figure who don't give two shits about ya'. It's as simple as that.

MIKE: Sam, it ain't as simple as that...

SAM: No, it is, Mike...

MIKE: Sam, you don't go along with those cops, none a' this exists, okay?

SAM: Mike, don't go there...

MIKE: You're still a cop. You don't lose your badge, you don't go to prison...

SAM: *(Over "go to prison...")* Mike, don't fuckin' turn the tables on me, okay? Don't even fuckin' try it! *(An intense pause.)* The long'n the short is 'at you're gonna' side with that asshole, n'that's a mistake 'cause lemme tell ya' somethin', my friend, I been around a little longer than you n'seen past my mother's kitchen, n'if there's one thing I've learned is 'at I wouldn't trust any of 'em as far as I can throw 'em. How far y'think you can throw Ernie?

> *(A still moment, as Mike is nearly stunned, before breaking into weak laughter...)*

MIKE: Shit, y'sound like my father.

SAM: Y'should give 'im a little more credit.

> *(A moment.)*

100

MIKE: Yeah, Sam, that's what I'll do. *(Rises...)* Y'know,...I think I'm gonna' go, okay?

SAM: *(Slight pause.)* So that's it?

MIKE: Yeah, man.

> *(They look at each other for a moment, and it is clear that SAM is strongly disappointed at this turn of events, before turning back to screen...)*

> *(MIKE motions to leave, before stopping...)*

Y'know, Sam, jus' so y'know, I still think most cops are good cops. I jus' don't think you were one of 'em.

> *(SAM looks at MIKE intensely for a moment...)*

SAM: Have a nice life, Mike.

> *(MIKE eventually exits...)*

> *(SAM looks off for a moment, sips, turns back to screen...)*

> *(Lights)*

> *(*As with the previous transition, with music, we see the final stages of the park being completed; all sodding, flowers, paths, etc. All in dim light, with the workers indistinguishable from one another, as before.)*

Scene 4

We hear sounds of applause, a crowd inaudibly conversing, departing, which fades out as the lights fade up on ERNIE and MIKE across from one another, but at a considerable distance. They are both wearing suits. We see the park complete.

101

It is Fall, about 5 months later.

A moment.

MIKE: 'sup.

ERNIE: *(Slight pause.)* Thought I saw ya' earlier, but I wasn't sure.

MIKE: The suit?

ERNIE: For starters, yeah.

MIKE: I know. I never wear suits.

ERNIE: I can tell.

MIKE: I gotta' get it taken in or somethin' when I get time. Looks like a fuckin' circus tent on me.

    (A moment.)

ERNIE: Y'workin'?

MIKE: Yeah. With a commercial company based in Red Hook.

ERNIE: Alright.

MIKE: Small. Not even full-time. I'm still lookin'.

ERNIE: Mhm.

    (A moment.)

MIKE: Got a place.

ERNIE: No shit.

MIKE: Yeah, man. Had t'get outa' that house. Enough was enough, y'know?

ERNIE: I know.

MIKE: Don't know how much longer I'll be able t'keep it with what I'm makin', but it's mine for now, so...

ERNIE: Cool.

MIKE: Surprised, I bet.

ERNIE: Not really. Thought you may end up movin' in with a girlfriend or somethin'.

MIKE: Nah. Thought about it. Darlene wanted me to but, it didn't feel right. If it don't work out between us, I'm back t'livin' at home, y'know? So I figured...

ERNIE: Yeah, I hear ya'.

(A moment.)

Still seein' the other one?

MIKE: Nah. That's done.

ERNIE: Who else now?

MIKE: No one else.

ERNIE: Jus' Darlene.

MIKE: Yeah, jus' Darlene.

ERNIE: Goin' okay?

MIKE: Okay enough, yeah. Who knows up the road. But it's okay. I like 'er.

ERNIE: Gonna' be with someone, y'may as well like 'em, right?

(A moment.)

MIKE: Sorry they didn't let ya' read.

ERNIE: Ah. Figured as much.

MIKE: Why? They said you could read, right? They sent you a letter, f'Godsakes...

ERNIE: They ran long. You know these politicians. They can yap until the sun sets, or at least until the cameras're turned off.

MIKE: Yeah, no kiddin'. Fuckin' guy's quotin' Maya Angelou. I'm like, what the hella' you quotin' her for. Y'got a poet right in fronta' ya'.

ERNIE: She's a poet. I'm a landscaper who likes writin' poetry. There's a difference.

MIKE: Well,... You're takin' it better than I would, if I could write for shit.

ERNIE: They meant well. Jus' fell through.

(A moment.)

Park turned out nice, huh?

MIKE: Yeah, awesome, man.

ERNIE: Just in time for the elections.

MIKE: Yeah, no shit. You guys should get a bonus for that.

ERNIE: Yeah, that'll happen.

MIKE: Seriously though, you guys did great work on it.

ERNIE: *(A beat.)* You had a hand.

MIKE: Eh, c'mon. I helped with excavation'n stuff but... You guys did the job.

ERNIE: It's the rose a' the neighborhood, that's for sure.

MIKE: You ain't kiddin'.

ERNIE: Let's hope they know how to treat it.

MIKE: Yeah, well... Who knows.

   (A considerable moment.)

ERNIE: I never told you much about my wife, did I.

MIKE: *(Slight pause.)* No.

ERNIE: Yeah, well... She was... She really got me in a way I didn't think any woman could. Smart, sweet, didn't take my shit, didn't suffer fools,... And one funny-ass woman, too. I mean, she'd make me piss myself sometimes, that's how damn funny she could be... Anyway, 7 years into us bein' married, she got sick. Fuckin' liver cancer. 32 years old. *(Slight pause.)* She needed a transplant, n'she was in line for one. But bein' in line for a liver is like bein' in line for a bar a' gold, y'know? It ain't like the kidneys, where everyone's got one t'spare. So we waited for someone t'die so she could live, until she couldn't keep livin' herself anymore. *(Slight pause.)* Somehow I found out that the liver that shoulda' gone t'her ended up goin' to some alcoholic sitcom actor. White dude. *(Slight pause.)* I found that out…n'it seemed like as soon as all the tears had left my ducts, they were replaced by my hatred a' every white sitcom actor I ever saw. *(Slight pause.)* Then every white actor. *(Slight pause.)* Then every white man. *(Pause.)* I was one bitter sonofabitch for a long time, Mike. Roberta was gone. Was never gonna' have the family we wanted,…n'all I had was myself t'look at n'it got t'where I was even hatin' that. So eventually I jus' started t'ease out a' that way a' thinkin'. Started to realize the energy I was expendin' on bein' so angry. So I stopped drinkin' too much, eatin' too much, even took up yoga, started writin'… Got my shit together n'jus'…began feelin' like life was here for me insteada' tryin' to fuck with me, y'know? *(Slight pause.)* But these feelings can come'n go like the breeze on any given day. And when they go,…all the namastes in the world can't much help. *(Slight pause.)* I guess we're all meant t'be tested in one way or another, or else we probably ain't alive.

(A moment. They look at each other.)

(Eventually, ERNIE moves to a nearby bench. He sits, gazes out,…and eventually taps the space next to him.)

(MIKE gradually makes his way over, sits. They gaze out.)

MIKE: Wana' read your poem?

ERNIE: *(Slight pause.)* Yeah?

MIKE: Yeah. I came all the way the fuck out here t'hear it, man. C'mon.

ERNIE: *(Slight pause.)* Alright. Well, God knows I wouldn't wana' have you waste the subway fare.

MIKE: Wana' stand?

ERNIE: No, I'm fine right where I am.

MIKE: Alright, I jus' thought…

ERNIE: *(Over "thought…")* I'm sittin', okay?

MIKE: Alright, fine. Sit.

> *(ERNIE pulls out a folded piece of paper from his jacket, along with reading glasses. He takes an authorly moment...)*

ERNIE: *Harmony Park* by Ernie Bennett.

> *From where mere pavement once stood,*
> *adorned in a fence clad with rust,*
> *men dug up these eroded grounds*
> *to create a haven from the dust.*
>
> *African violets and lilacs*
> *now stand together as one*
> *with periwinkle and hedera helix*
> *in a garden beneath the sun.*
>
> *From a sculpted angel fountain,*
> *tranquil water streams below,*
> *baptizing many a mulberry bush*
> *and the winding path of stones.*

2 girls of aspiration,
one black, one white,
so much of life before them,
so much within their sights.

I can even say with candor
that there were days I stood alone,
saddened by why this had to be,
as if those two girls were my own.
But today, I can almost smile
at the work done from day to dark,
for this new Eden belongs to two young spirits,
and to all who visit...Harmony Park.

(ERNIE takes a moment to remain in the character of a
poet, before quickly folding the paper, and placing his
glasses back in his pocket.)

ERNIE: So there y'go.

(He faces out, as does MIKE, who is moved.)

(They both continue to gaze out, before MIKE turns to
ERNIE, nods approvingly,...as if words fail.)

(They look at each other.)

(Lights)

End of Play

THE GOLDEN YEAR

THE GOLDEN YEAR

The Golden Year received its World Premiere with the WorkShop Theater Company in New York City, with the following cast and production staff, June 2013:

JEAN……………………….……..Ellen Barry
JOE………...…………….....…Gerry Goodstein
JEREMY………………………Joseph Franchini

Directed by Kathy Gail MacGowan

Stage Manager: Genevieve Ortiz
Lighting Designer: Kia Rogers
Sound Designer: Julian Evans
Set Designer: Will Lowry
Press: Scott Rhodes Publicity
Associate Producer: Cecily Benjamin Hughes
Producing Director: Delisa M. White
Artistic Director: Scott Sickles

Special Thanks to the following artists who lent their talents to previous readings of *The Golden Year*:

Ken Glickfeld, Richard Kent Green, Kathryn Kates
and Gerrianne Raphael.

Cast of Characters

JOE BRANCATO – *Mid-to-late 60's. Husband to Jean.*
JEAN BRANCATO – *Mid-to-late 60's. Wife to Joe.*
JEREMY LEVITICUS – *30s-40s.*

Various Pre-Recorded Voices.

The home of Joe & Jean Brancato in the town of Packinsau (Long Island, New York).

2013

The play should be performed without intermission.

Scene 1

JEAN & JOE sit in their recliners, facing out. Game-show buzzers and rings faintly emanate from an unseen TV. It is apparent that JOE's comfort is a contrast to JEAN.

A moment.

JEAN: I don't know what to do with myself.

JOE: *(Slight pause.)* Whata' y'have to do?

JEAN: Well, I just can't sit around.

JOE: Why not?

JEAN: Why not?

JOE: Jean, it's the privilege of retirement.

JEAN: It should be more liberating than *this*.

JOE: There's liberation in doing nothing.

JEAN: Joe, this is too much of nothing.

JOE: *(Slight pause.)* We have the rest of our lives to go away places. We just stopped working, for Godsakes.

JEAN: I'm aware.

JOE: Okay, so…

JEAN: Because I'm old.

JOE: Jean,…

JEAN: That's how they penalize you in this country. God forbid you're old.

JOE: Jean,…

JEAN: God forbid a gray hair.

JOE: Jean,…

JEAN: God forbid a wrinkle…

JOE: Honey, you were too good for that place. You know that.

JEAN: Too good for a place I worked at for 27 years.

> *(JOE turns off TV with remote…)*

JOE: You gave them everything you could, and they were damn lucky to have you when they did. Now they can go to hell. Alright? It's just as well. This is what we've worked for.

JEAN: I understand, dear.

JOE: You can *afford* to retire.

JEAN: I know.

JOE: So many people in this country *have* to work, even at our age. But look at us.

JEAN: Joe,…

JOE: We got our investments. The house is finally paid up. We got our health.

JEAN: Thank God.

JOE: Thank God is right. *(Slight pause, as he faces out.)* We'll go away soon, just like we've always said we'd do. For now, we're just takin' it easy. There's nothin' wrong with that.

> *(JOE turns back on TV.)*

> *(A moment.)*

JEAN: It's just…

> *(JOE turns off TV…)*

JOE: What?

JEAN: I'm afraid I'm just not over it.

JOE: Over what?

JEAN: It was embarrassing. To be forced.

JOE: Jean,…

JEAN: For you, it was a choice, at least.

JOE: Well, that was different.

JEAN: Because you're a man.

JOE: Because I worked a different type of job. A different industry. Different responsibilities. I had people under me. It was different, Jean.

JEAN: *(Slight pause.)* You really wanted to stop?

JOE: What, are you kiddin'? *You're* the one who wanted to keep workin'. Jesus, I wanted to retire years ago. I mean, yeah, if you still had your job, I mighta' stayed another year or so, but it worked out. My God, I was long done with that place. You know that.

> *(A moment.)*

JEAN: Joe.

JOE: Yes?

JEAN: You feel…?

JOE: *(Slight pause.)* Yes?

JEAN: You feel as if you were doing what you wanted to do? All those years?

JOE: At the office?

JEAN: Yeah.

JOE: More-or-less, yeah.

JEAN: You worked your way up. You put in a lot of hours. You felt respected.

JOE: Yeah.

> *(A moment. JOE turns on TV.)*

> *(A moment.)*

JEAN: Joe?

> *(JOE turns off TV ...)*

JOE: Yes?

JEAN: *(Slight pause.)* I don't feel I've fulfilled my potential.

JOE: How's that?

JEAN: I feel I haven't done what I've really wanted to do.

JOE: As a career?

JEAN: In life.

JOE: What?

JEAN: I'm serious, Joe. *(Slight pause.)* Alluvasudden, I feel like I haven't lived a day.

JOE: Jesus Christ, Jean, how can you say that?

JEAN: I just did.

JOE: What, you've lived. We've lived.

JEAN: We've had a nice marriage, Joe, but *you've* lived.

JOE: Oh, Jeez Louise...

JEAN: More than me.

JOE: C'mon, honey…

JEAN: You've done what you wanted to do. You wanted to work. You wanted to leave. Now you want to do nothing.

JOE: You've done things.

JEAN: What?

JOE: What, the kids?

JEAN: That's giving birth, Joe. That's not living. That's not experiencing life.

JOE: Isn't giving life part of experiencing life?

JEAN: No, because once they left my body, they had lives of their own. Their own experiences. I mean, I love them, Joe, but it's…it's just…

JOE: What?

JEAN: It's just…not the same.

JOE: Jesus, you make it like…

JEAN: What?

JOE: I mean, how could you live and work every day of your life and then one day, out of the blue, say you've done nothing? That's ridiculous.

JEAN: It's called reflection. That's what we do when we get older. We look back. We see how we could've made more of our time.

JOE: And so now you see us sitting comfortably in our living room and you can't stand it.

JEAN: Joe,…

JOE: All I want to do is nothing for just a coupla' months before embarking on all our adventures, and you can't sit still because you have this delusion that you've done nothing with your life.

JEAN: I didn't say I've… C'mon, honey. I don't regret our marriage…or the kids…

JOE: Alright, good.

JEAN: Even if they hardly call.

JOE: Don't take that personally.

JEAN: How can I not? They're our children.

JOE: Younger generations are more self-involved. You know that.

JEAN: Christ, that's not even the issue.

JOE: Right. You've done nothing.

JEAN: I just… I have the right to feel a discontent.

JOE: *(Slight pause, smiles.)* Once we cash out everything, we'll see the world. Just like we talked about. Okay?

JEAN: *(Slight pause, an appeasing smile.)* Alright.

JOE: Jesus, we've barely been out of the state, let alone the country. Are you kiddin'?

JEAN: I know.

JOE: Our whole lives, workin'.

JEAN: I know.

JOE: God, I can't wait to go to Italy, Ireland, Egypt…

JEAN: *(A beat, momentarily transported…)* The Great Wall of China.

JOE: *(Similarly...)* The Eiffel Tower.

JEAN: The Louvre.

JOE: The Vatican.

JEAN: That beautiful ceiling.

JOE: Sure, are you kiddin'?

JEAN: How nice.

JOE: Y'see? We'll do it all. We got our legs, our health...

JEAN: Thank God.

JOE: Thank God is right.

> *(JEAN and JOE look at each other. JEAN extends her hand, which he takes.)*

> *(After a beat, JOE, with his other hand, subtly turns on TV...)*

> *(A moment.)*

JEAN: But still.

> *(JOE turns off TV...)*

JOE: *(Slight pause.)* What?

JEAN: That's not everything.

JOE: What's not?

JEAN: Traveling. It's a diversion.

JOE: That's what traveling is. It's a diversion.

JEAN: But I don't want the rest of my life to be a diversion, Joe.

JOE: You said you wanted to travel.

JEAN: Well, of course. Doesn't everybody?

JOE: And we will.

JEAN: But it's still…

JOE: *(A beat.)* What?

JEAN: It still wouldn't fill something.

JOE: Fill what?

JEAN: Joe,…

JOE: Honey, what? Fill what? You're talkin' hieroglyphics to me here.

JEAN: A void.

JOE: A void.

JEAN: Within me. What I haven't done.

JOE: You've done plenty.

JEAN: What've I done?

JOE: What, you worked, you raised the kids…

JEAN: Joe, that's not enough. I've been in denial about…about something.

JOE: What?

JEAN: I've suppressed things.

JOE: What things?

JEAN: Oh, God, I don't even remember anymore… Oh, God, Joe…!

JOE: Honey,…

JEAN: *(In a near panic…)* …oh, God, Joe…!

119

JOE: Honey, you're overwhelming yourself, okay?

JEAN: *(Slight pause, gathers somewhat.)* I'm sorry.

JOE: Don't be sorry. Just calm down, okay? My God, I've never seen you like...

JEAN: I don't know what's come over me, alluvasudden.

JOE: *(Slight pause, attempting to elevate.)* You know what this is? You're making yourself feel guilty for not working anymore. You've worked your whole life and your body hasn't adjusted. I've read about this.

JEAN: You've *read* about it?

JOE: Yeah, an article or somethin' about how people adapt to change. There's always a...whata' they say, like a natural trepidation. 'cause, y'know, it's unchartered waters, right? The unknown. I mean, you've never not worked before. You've never had a whole day to just...do nothing. It's new. So that's the process you're going through; learning to do nothing.

JEAN: But...

JOE: You'll be fine, honey. We've known each other how long?

JEAN: *(Slight pause.)* My God, over 40 years.

JOE: You've always been fine. And when something's ruffled your feathers, you've gotten over it. And you've been stronger for it.

JEAN: I...

JOE: It's one of your greatest attributes.

JEAN: *(Timidly.)* Is it?

JOE: Of course. My God, honey, I've never heard you doubt yourself like this.

JEAN: I guess I just...

JOE: *(Slight pause.)* What?

JEAN: *(Slight pause, softly.)* Nothing.

JOE: *(Slight pause.)* Everything'll be great. Okay? Hey, this is the start of our Golden Years, right? Y'think they call it that for nothin'?

JEAN: *(A half smile.)* Hm.

JOE: *(A boisterous chuckle...)* Huh? Are you kiddin'? We got wonderful things ahead of us, honey,...and, knock wood, we've got our good health to enjoy it with.

JEAN: *(Weakly...)* Thank God.

JOE: Thank God is right.

> *(JOE extends his hand to JEAN, which she takes. They look out, as before. JOE again, subtly, takes remote and turns on TV...)*

> *(A moment.)*

JEAN: But still.

> *(JEAN gazes out, as JOE looks at her.)*

> *(Lights)*

Scene 2

Two weeks later, living room. JOE sits. JEAN stands, with newspaper in hand...

JOE: You're kidding.

JEAN: Nope. I'm doin' it.

JOE: Wow. That's...

JEAN: Isn't that something?

JOE: Yeah, it's…it's something, Jean. I… Wow.

JEAN: I mean, why the hell not?

JOE: Well,…

JEAN: I'm jus' gonna' try it.

JOE: I mean…

JEAN: I probably won't even get chosen, but who knows, right?

JOE: You sure you wana' do this?

JEAN: Well, why not? It's something I've always been curious about.

JOE: Acting?

JEAN: I mentioned it to you before.

JOE: Before when? I don't remember you mentioning that.

JEAN: I'm sure I did. I mean, it would've been years ago. Anyway, it's always been something I've found interesting, y'know? And now I have the time, right?

JOE: I…well, yeah…

JEAN: I mean, we weren't gonna' go away tomorrow, right?

JOE: Well, maybe not…

JEAN: But I mean, Joe, I'm not even chosen yet. Who's to say I'll even get picked.

JOE: No, I know…

JEAN: I just figured I have the time, it seems like fun, so…

JOE: Alright, honey. If it's something you wana' try, I'm behind ya'.

JEAN: Really?

JOE: Well, God, I know you've been sorta' climbing the walls lately, so…

JEAN: Thank you, honey. Again, nothin' may come of it but…

JOE: It's just… Y'know.

JEAN: *(A beat.)* What?

JOE: Well, I just… Are you gonna' be okay if you don't get selected?

JEAN: Well, sure. Why?

JOE: I'm jus' sayin'. Because, y'know, I know you're still sorta' lickin' your wounds. I just…

JEAN: Oh, honey, this isn't like that.

JOE: Well,…

JEAN: Oh, please. My God, I haven't even acted,…unless you count the time I played a celery stick in the 1st grade. I never even took drama in high school, for Godsakes, because my mother thought it was wasteful. I've just always felt there was some-thing…I don't know…

JOE: What?

JEAN: I dunno, something sort of emotionally cathartic about acting. I mean, we've seen those Acting Studio shows on TV.

JOE: Oh, God, I hate that uppity sonofabitch, Jean.

JEAN: No, not the host. The actors; they always talk about how they…they use their characters to channel their emotions in a healthy way. I mean,…that's wonderful. I just thought this'd be therapeutic for me.

JOE: I understand, honey. I'm jus' sayin'…what'll it be for you if you don't get in?

JEAN: Whata' y'mean?

JOE: It's therapeutic and cathartic'n all that if you get the part. What if y'don't? That's what I'm worried about, honey…

JEAN: Oh, Joe, I'll be fine. I just really wana' try this.

JOE: Okay, honey…

JEAN: And who knows, right? We've seen some of the stuff they've done at that theatre over the years.

JOE: Yeah, I know.

JEAN: My God, we saw that awful production last summer of… oh God, what the hell was it? We saw it because your proctologist was in it. With the couple.

JOE: *Same Time Tomorrow*?

JEAN: *Next Year*.

JOE: What was it?

JEAN: *Same Time, Next Year*.

JOE: Oh, right. That was okay, actually.

JEAN: I could've done better than she did.

JOE: It's not like she was a professional.

JEAN: That's what I'm sayin'. I think she was a Librarian, for Godsakes.

JOE: Well, it's community theatre, honey.

JEAN: Exactly. And I'm part of the community, right?

JOE: Alright, honey…

JEAN: So why not?

JOE: Okay, honey…

JEAN: And it scares me.

JOE: Scares you?

JEAN: The prospect of auditioning, the whole experience. It scares the livin' hell outa' me, Joe, and I think that's fabulous.

JOE: Fabulous?

JEAN: Yeah. I mean, Joe, I've been looking at these audition ads for years. And I've always thought to myself, "Hey, what if?" But I was workin', I was scared, I was this'n that... But it's like you said, about...about venturing into "unchartered waters". Adapting. Except in this case it's not about adapting to doing nothing. It's adapting to doing something I've never done before.

JOE: Okay, honey...

JEAN: Hell, why don't you audition too?

JOE: What?!

JEAN: The Husband. The Grandfather part. Why not? You're not doing anything tomorrow afternoon.

JOE: Jean, are you...?

JEAN: You're exactly in the age range they're looking for...

JOE: Are you outa' your mind?

JEAN: Why not?

JOE: Jean, absolutely not.

JEAN: Oh, come on. You're perfect for it.

JOE: Jean, just because we're the similar age doesn't mean I can act. I've never been on a stage in my life. What, y'wana' give me a heart attack?

JEAN: I just think this'd be a fun thing for us to do together.

JOE: Honey, in this case, I'll live vicariously through you. Okay?

JEAN: *(A beat.)* Alright.

>*(JEAN sits in her chair, beside JOE.)*

>*(A moment, as they face out.)*

Will you help me with my lines?

JOE: Your what?

JEAN: If I get the part, will you help me learn my lines? Y'know, say the lines of the other parts so I can learn mine?

JOE: *(A beat, an indulgent smile.)* Sure, honey.

>*(A moment.)*

JEAN: I mean, again, I probably won't even get the part, but…stranger things've happened.

>*(JEAN smiles.)*

>*(Lights)*

Scene 3

An outgoing phone ring into an exclusive light on JOE, standing, with cordless phone. Next day, afternoon.

JOE: Yeah, hiya' there, Barry. This is Joe. Joe Brancato. I don't know if you're checking messages. You don't say on your outgoing message when you're due back, so I figured I'd just try ya' again, since it's been a few weeks. Anyway, as I mentioned before – Hello? Hello? Shit.

>*(He hangs up, hits redial…)*

Yeah, hiya', Barry! Joe. Joe Brancato again. I guess I took up too much time on your machine there. Anyway, again, if you're back in town or if you're checking messages, if you wouldn't

mind, I'd – Hello? Hello? *(Slight pause, as he looks at phone.)*
Shit.

> *(Lights)*

Scene 4

*An exclusive light on JEAN with a page in hand. She is nervous,
and reads crudely but with a certain conviction, accompanied
by overtly-grand gestures throughout...*

JEAN: *"For the life a' me, Morris, I don't know why he did what
he did. He had everything. I know he didn't think that, with losin'
his job and the Crash'n all...but he had Dolores. He had our
grandchildren, Leonard and Theresa. He had us. Oh, dear God
in Heaven, why couldn't...why couldn't he just see the forest for
the trees? Why could he not see that, despite everything, despite
how bleak everything looked, there was a light at the end of the
tunnel. I believed it, Morris. I know everyone looked at me crazy
when I said that, but I believed this. Maybe I was wrong. Maybe
we're all fated to live hand-to-mouth for the rest of our days but,
my God, Morris, let the Lord take us when he's ready. Not because we've given up. He was our son, Morris. He was our only
son!"*

> *(She looks out, as if seeking the approval, then back at
> page, then out again...)*

JEAN: That's all that's here.

> *(Lights)*

Scene 5

*In darkness, the faint sounds of water dripping, before lights
come up. JOE sits, JEAN stands. Living room. Later afternoon.*

JEAN: I got it!

JOE: What?

JEAN: I got the part!

JOE: You're kiddin'. You got the part?

JEAN: The Grandmother part.

JOE: Yeah…

JEAN: Joe, I can't believe it.

JOE: That's…wow, Jean…

JEAN: I'm…, oh my God, Joe…

JOE: *(Rises…)* It's okay…

JEAN: Oh my God…

JOE: Well, sit down already.

JEAN: *(As she excitedly sits, then immediately stands…)* They were gonna' wait because they usually have what they call "callbacks".

JOE: Yeah, okay.

JEAN: Like a second interview.

JOE: I got it, yeah…

JEAN: But they cast me right on the spot. 17 other women up for the same role and I was the last one seen, and they cast me right then and there, Joe.

JOE: Looka' that.

JEAN: Isn't that something'?

JOE: Outa' 17 women?

JEAN: 17, Joe!

JOE: Looka' that!

JEAN: Oh, and Dr. Filbert sends his best.

JOE: My proctologist?

JEAN: Yeah, he was auditioning too.

JOE: Oh. Well, he's a pretty good actor himself.

JEAN: Yeah, he is. We even read together.

JOE: Oh, yeah?

JEAN: Joe, I'm so excited!

JOE: I know!

JEAN: Isn't this something? Who'da' thought, right?

JOE: I'm stunned.

JEAN: *(A beat.)* Stunned?

JOE: Well, come on, Jean, I've never seen you act before n'al-luvasudden your... God, look at ya'. You're a star, for Godsakes!

JEAN: Oh, stop. It's a supporting role.

JOE: That's alright.

JEAN: But I have some wonderful scenes, and some very nice speeches, from what I read.

JOE: Great.

JEAN: It seems like a very powerful play.

JOE: What's it called?

JEAN: *Plight of the Longshoreman.*

JOE: *Plight of the Longshoreman...*

JEAN: It won their New Play Contest, which the Packinsau Players just started this summer. The writer is 82, lives in town. A retired lawyer, believe it or not.

JOE: Okay.

JEAN: Basically the plays had to be about a point in American History, and so his was the Great Depression.

JOE: So what's it about?

JEAN: Well, I haven't read it, except for the coupla' scenes they had me read, but from what they told me, it's about this family in New York City right after the Crash.

JOE: Okay.

JEAN: There's the Grandmother, Grandfather, their son, their daughter-in-law and their 2 grandchildren. The father and son are the main characters, because the son loses his job and the father, my husband, ends up supporting the whole household...

JOE: Wow. Sounds interesting.

JEAN: Very dramatic.

JOE: Yeah, real meat'n potatoes, huh?

JEAN: I'm gonna' read through the script in bed, okay?

JOE: Uh,...yeah, sure.

(As JEAN starts off...)

JEAN: Anything interesting happen here this afternoon?

JOE: Nah, just relaxed. Oh, and we got a leak in the bathroom now.

JEAN: A leak?

JOE: Yeah. From the ceiling. Alluvasudden.

JEAN: Where?

JOE: Over the shower.

JEAN: I didn't notice it.

JOE: Yeah, well, we have it. Alluvasudden.

JEAN: So what, do we have to call the roofers?

JOE: No, it's gotta' be a plumbing thing.

JEAN: What, you think it's a pipe?

JOE: It has to be. It hasn't rained in weeks. How else are we gettin' a leak in the ceiling?

JEAN: Well, I don't know, Joe. I'm just sayin'…

JOE: It's a pipe. This is an old house, so it probably needs a little tweaking.

JEAN: Alright, well, did you call the plumber?

JOE: Called three guys. The earliest someone can get here is next week. *(…as he sits.)*

JEAN: Did you call our broker, like y'said?

JOE: *(Slight pause.)* Yeah. Left a coupla' messages.

JEAN: Still on vacation?

JOE: Yeah, I guess.

JEAN: My God, where'd he go?

JOE: Where? He's on vacation. I don't know where. He'll be back soon enough.

JEAN: Well, Jesus, has he even called you back?

JOE: I told ya' he did.

JEAN: When?

JOE: I told ya'. A few weeks ago. Right before I stopped working he left a message on my office voicemail that it'd be his top priority when he got back. He just didn't say when. He's a busy man, Jean.

JEAN: I just think it'd be nice if he…

JOE: *(Eagerly, as he rises…)* Honey, I got it under control. I know this guy 10 years. Right now, let's just enjoy your new success, huh? Look at ya', you're Jessica Tandy, for cryin' out loud!

JEAN: *(A beat, an indulgent smile.)* Thank you for supporting me in this, Joe.

JOE: And if I didn't, you'd a' done it anyway.

JEAN: Well, I know it sounded like a fluke thing but….

JOE: I'm proud of ya', honey.

JEAN: You are?

JOE: I've always been.

JEAN: Oh, Joe, but this is…this is really… *(Containing her almost girlish enthusiasm.)* Thank you, honey.

> *(They kiss.)*

See ya' later.

> *(JEAN eagerly exits, clutching script, as JOE sits in his chair. He smiles while looking out, before he takes remote and turns on the unseen TV…)*

VOICE OF METEOROLOGIST: *…mild winds coming in from the west with temperatures from a low of 75 to a mere high of 80. The glorious absence of humidity continues as we take a look at our 7-day forecast, courtesy of our Doppler radar. As you can see, temperatures will remain more-or-less the same through the weekend…*

(Lights fade into the slightly louder sound of water dripping...)

Scene 6

Lights up on JEAN in living room, with script in hand. Two days later, late morning.

JEAN: Joe? *(Waits.)* Joe?! *(Waits.)* Joe, are you okay?!

JOE: *(Offstage.)* What?!

JEAN: Oh, my God. I thought you flushed yourself.

JOE: *(Offstage.)* What?!

JEAN: Are you okay?!

(JOE comes on.)

JOE: What?

JEAN: Are you...? What happened?

JOE: Whata' y'mean? I was in the bathroom.

JEAN: For over an hour.

JOE: Was I?

JEAN: Are you okay?

JOE: Yeah, I'm okay. Why?

JEAN: You weren't trying to fix that leak yourself.

JOE: I told ya' the guy's comin' next week.

JEAN: So what were ya' doin' in there for an hour?

JOE: What, I musta' gotten carried away with the crosswords or somethin'.

JEAN: Jeez, you usually do those in minutes.

JOE: Well, whata' y'gonna' do. Maybe I'm losin' my touch.

(...as JOE sits in chair, grabs nearby paper...)

JEAN: So are y'ready?

JOE: Ready for what?

JEAN: You were gonna' help me with my lines, remember? We have our first rehearsal on Monday and I wana' start learning my lines.

JOE: How soon do they want you to know your lines? You've had the part 2 days.

JEAN: Well, I want to be as prepared as I can be.

JOE: *(A beat.)* Alright, well give me the book.

JEAN: Joe, are you kidding? I don't know my lines yet. I just want to run them with you.

JOE: You don't have an extra copy?

JEAN: No, they only gave me the one.

JOE: So how are we gonna' do this?

JEAN: We'll just share. I'll sit on the arm a' the chair.

(JOE sits with book, JEAN beside him...)

JOE: Okay, so you want me to read...?

JEAN: Just read the stage directions and all the other characters in my scenes.

JOE: How many characters?

JEAN: I'm only in 4 scenes, mainly with the son and then with my husband.

JOE: You don't want me to do voices or anything, do ya'...?

JEAN: No, just read them straight.

JOE: Okay, here y'go. Y'ready?

JEAN: Thank you, dear. Yes.

JOE: Alright. *"Plight of the Longshoreman*, Act 1, Scene 1..."

JEAN: Read these stage directions too.

JOE: All this?

JEAN: Yeah.

JOE: Why do ya' need me to read that? You're lookin' at it with me.

JEAN: I want to picture it in my mind and not see it on the page. I need to start imagining it.

JOE: *(A beat.)* Alright.

JEAN: Okay?

JOE: Okay, here we go;

> *(*Throughout the stage directions, Jean attempts to subtly enact the characteristics Joe reads...)*

JOE: *"The cramped residence of Morris and Estelle Mankowitz, New York City, 1929. Estelle, a woman in her late 60's, enters. She is aged, worn down via the struggles of daily life, but perpetually hopeful. She clears up plates from the morning's breakfast, before her son, Tobas, enters..."*

JEAN: Tobias.

JOE: What?

JEAN: Tobias.

JOE: It says *"Tobas"*...

JEAN: It's a typo. He forgot the "i" there.

JOE: *"**Tobias** enters; a man in his 30's, unusually lugubrious this morning."*

JEAN: *(Overtly grand, as earlier.)* *"Tobias, what are you doing home?"* Then there's a pause, he doesn't answer. *"Tobias?"* Now you read…

JOE: *(Flatly, with volume, but without emotional resonance.)* *"They cut me."*

JEAN: *"Cut you! Are you hurt?!"*

JOE: *"No, they let me go, ma. They laid off 30 of us this morning, and I was one of 'em."*

JEAN: *"Oh, dear God."*

JOE: *"I can't believe it."*

JEAN: *"You go all the way down there to work and **then** they tell ya'?"*

JOE: *"How else were they gonna' tell me, ma? We don't have a phone."*

JEAN: *"Well, it'll be fine. It's worked out before and it'll work out again."*

JOE: *"Except it hasn't worked out. Just when you think it works out, I lose another job."*

JEAN: *"Tobias, these are hard times, we're livin' in…"*

JOE: *"I know what times it is, ma. It's a hard time to have a job. It's a hard time to have a family. It's a hard time to have anything, let alone a dream."*

> *(Phone rings…)*

Hold on. It might be…

(JOE picks up…)

Hello. Joe Brancato. – Who? - *Leviticus…?*

JEAN: That's for me?

JOE: For *you?*

JEAN: Jeremy Leviticus. He's our director. Let me have…

JOE: Alright, here…

(JEAN eagerly takes phone…)

JEAN: Hello, Jeremy? – Yes, this is Jean. How are you? - Yes, I've read it over several times. I'm even running lines with my husband as we speak. – Okay. – Yes, I have it written in my book; next Monday at 6pm at the community center. – Okay. – Thanks for the reminder. – See ya' then. *(Hangs up.)* That was the director.

JOE: Yeah, I know.

JEAN: He was just reminding me about our first rehearsal.

JOE: Why does he have to remind ya'? They already told ya', right?

JEAN: He told me, he e-mailed me. He's apparently a perfectionist.

JOE: Oh, yeah?

JEAN: Dr. Filbert told me that at the audition. He did *Last of the Red Hot Lovers* with him a few years ago. Said he was brilliant, but a little anal retentive.

JOE: Gee, with Filbert being a proctologist, you'd think he'd prefer that.

JEAN: Oh, stop.

JOE: *(With a slight smile…)* Oh come on. He loves those ass jokes.

JEAN: I told you he's in the cast too, right?

JOE: Who, Filbert?

JEAN: Yeah.

JOE: Who's he playing? The son?

JEAN: The son? What am I, an artifact, Joe? He's playing my husband.

JOE: Your husband.

JEAN: Yeah.

JOE: Well, the guy's in his late 50s at best.

JEAN: Alright, so.

JOE: Couldn't they get someone your own age?

JEAN: Apparently, they couldn't find anyone as good. Plus the director's worked with him'n all that. It's the Theatre, Joe. They'll just add some more gray, he'll walk a little slower or whatever.

JOE: Alright, I just think it's funny.

JEAN: He's a good actor, Joe. I'm sure he'll be believable.

JOE: No, I'm not sayin' that. I'm just sayin'…my proctologist is your husband.

JEAN: *Stage* husband.

JOE: Yeah, I know. It's just funny, don't y'think?

JEAN: *(A beat.)* It is a little funny, isn't it.

    (They share a laugh…)

Alright, let's get back to the play.

JOE: What, we can laugh.

JEAN: And we did. Now let's not dilly-dally. Let's take it from where we left off. With the son.

JOE: Alright, alright. Hold your horses. Here we go. *(With his usual flat delivery…)* *"I know what times it is, ma. It's a hard time to have a job. It's a hard time to have a family. It's a hard time to have anything, let alone a dream."*

JEAN: *"Don't say such a thing, Tobias!"*

JOE: *"It's true, ma. Look at how we're livin', the six of us crammed into a matchbox apartment."*

JEAN: *"What's true is believing in your dreams. Believing that God will shine his light on us."*

JOE: *"Ma, …"*

(Phone rings. Again, JOE urgently reaches for it…)

JOE: Hello. Joe Brancato. – Who? – Dr. Filbert? – Yeah, it's Joe. How are ya', Doc? - Yeah, the movements…seem to be moving along, as they should. Thanks for askin'. But I take it you're not calling to ask me *that*, right? – Yeah, okay. She's right here. – Yeah, I'm very much looking forward to it. She's very excited about this. – Alright, well here she is. Take care, Doc.

(Hands phone to JEAN…)

JEAN: Hello? – Hi, Doctor. What a coincidence. I just got off the phone with Jeremy. – Oh, well that's very nice of you, but I can drive myself, thanks. We have… – Oh, I see. Yeah, well, that sounds like a nice idea, so long as it isn't any inconvenience. – Okay, well, thank you, Doctor. You have our address, right…? – Alright, well I'll see you on Monday. – Take care.

(Hands phone to JOE, who hangs up…)

JOE: What's all that about?

JEAN: He wanted to give me a ride to rehearsal.

JOE: What, I can take ya' if you don't want to drive, Jean.

JEAN: No, it's not that. It's part of his method.

JOE: *(Slight pause.)* Whata' y'mean, his "method"?

JEAN: He's giving everyone a ride, because we're supposed to be a family, so he wants to create a certain…environment where, I guess, we're all a little more familiar with each other.

JOE: How familiar do ya' need to be?

JEAN: Whata' y'mean?

JOE: I've been his patient for almost 20 years. He's met you enough times.

JEAN: That's as a doctor, Joe. Not as an actor.

JOE: *(Rolling his eyes…)* Alright.

JEAN: I think it's very professional. It's just like something those actors on the Acting Studio show talk about. They do stuff like this.

JOE: Yeah, n'they also get paid millions a' dollars to do it.

JEAN: Joe, it's still art, regardless of what anyone's getting paid. I'm not saying it's necessary for me, but I'm open. I mean, he's done this before. I played a celery stick, for Godsakes.

JOE: So I guess if *he* played a celery stick, he'd be sleeping in the produce aisle?

JEAN: Joe…

JOE: *(He snorts a laugh…)* Alright, I'm sorry. Obviously, I respect the man as a doctor. I just find it a little ridiculous…

JEAN: I know it seems odd, but just indulge me, okay?

JOE: Alright.

JEAN: There's something to be said for being my age and doing something you've never done before.

JOE: Okay.

JEAN: Going against your instincts, y'know?

JOE: Alright,…

JEAN: I feel like this is the first time in years I'm leaving myself open to things.

JOE: *(Slight pause, a sincere smile.)* Okay, honey.

JEAN: Thank you, dear. *(She kisses his forehead…)* Let me get a glass a' water. I'm getting hoarse already. Y'want anything from the kitchen?

JOE: No, I'm good.

> *(JEAN exits off…)*

JEAN: Remember where we left off!

JOE: Sure. *(A beat, as he looks at script…)* *"What's true is believing in your dreams. Believing that God will shine his light on us."*

> *(Lights fade out and into…)*

Voice of BARRY ATKINSON: *"Hi, you've reached the office of Barry Atkinson. I'm currently away from my desk, so please leave a detailed message and I'll contact you at my earliest convenience. Thank you."*

> BEEP!

Automated Voice: *Mailbox is Full.*

Scene 7

Monday evening. The lights come up to reveal JOE (in bathrobe) sitting in his chair, pensively. He gazes at the unseen television, which emits a barely audible news broadcast...

The front door opening is heard... JEAN enters living room...

JEAN: You're still up?

JOE: I'm not gonna' go to bed before you're home.

JEAN: Is everything alright?

JOE: Yeah, fine. How was rehearsal?

JEAN: Oh, Joe, what fun it was tonight.

JOE: *(Indulging, mutes TV.)* Yeah?

JEAN: We just read through the script. What they call a "Table read". Just read through it, talked about it, but it was just so nice to hear everyone.

JOE: Good.

JEAN: Everyone is so talented in this cast, Joe.

JOE: Can't wait to see it.

JEAN: Well, you've got a few weeks yet. Thank God. Jesus, I had butterflies just sitting at the table tonight.

JOE: You'll be fine.

JEAN: And this speech I have at the end...

JOE: Oh, yeah?

JEAN: Joe, the play ends with me giving this...this...

JOE: Speech.

JEAN: Monologue. That's what they call it. Oh, my God, as soon as we get through the dialogue scenes, Joe, I'm gonna' need your help with it.

JOE: Alright, well…

JEAN: Anyway, I'm wiped out from all the excitement. Are you comin' to bed?

JOE: I'll be there in a bit.

JEAN: When're you coming to bed these days? I'm always out like a light.

JOE: I dunno', honey. I get there when I get there.

JEAN: You just look like you haven't been sleeping well.

JOE: Not particularly, but I'm alright.

JEAN: Well, why do you think that is?

JOE: I dunno', honey. It just is.

JEAN: Maybe some warm milk?

JOE: No, it'll bother my stomach.

JEAN: You haven't been drinking coffee too late, right?

JOE: The same time, as always.

JEAN: Hm. Well, y'know, Joe, maybe you're starting to get a little restless. You know, doing nothing. Maybe you may wana' do something.

JOE: Do what, honey? I just retired.

JEAN: A hobby.

JOE: I don't have hobbies, Jean. Work was my hobby, and I'm done with it.

JEAN: Well, maybe you're subconsciously itching to do something else, y'know?

(...as JOE rises, goes to window...)

JOE: Jean, I'm content to just do what I'm doing. Okay? There's the garden. That keeps me as busy as I wana' be.

JEAN: Whata' y'have to do about the garden? Everything's seeded. Takes ya' 20 minutes to water it. Nothing's ready to be picked.

JOE: There's the raccoons. They're keepin' me more active than ever. My God, I even had to scoot away a few tonight.

JEAN: I'm just sayin', something else to do might....

JOE: When we start traveling, that'll be something to do. I'm fine, honey.

JEAN: *(Slight pause.)* You're sure?

JOE: *(Slight pause, a forced smile.)* I'll be to bed in a bit.

JEAN: *(A beat.)* Okay.

(They kiss. JEAN starts to go off...)

Run lines with me after breakfast?

JOE: *(Slight pause, smiles.)* Sure, honey.

(JEAN exits. JOE sits back in chair, gazes at TV...)

(After a moment, he notices something crawling on the floor before him...)

What the hell...?

(He follows its sudden motions...before promptly stepping on it. Lights.)

Scene 8

The sounds of the following morning. JOE sits in his bathrobe with JEAN's play in hand, gazing out, while JEAN stands in an odd sort of statuesque character pose…

JEAN: *"Morris, do you remember when we met?" (No response.)* Morris? *(No response, turns to Joe.)* Joe?

JOE: *(Snapping out of it…)* Oh, sorry, hon…I was… Where are we here?

JEAN: That's the 3rd time, Joe.

JOE: I just went away there for a minute. I'm alright.

JEAN: Did you get any sleep last night?

JOE: I'm fine. Go ahead.

JEAN: What're you thinkin' about?

JOE: Nothing.

JEAN: You're obviously thinking about something.

JOE: The plumber's coming today, so I'm a little distracted, okay?

JEAN: Why is that distracting you? He's not coming until this afternoon.

JOE: I was thinking about it, Jean. Okay? Come on. Let's go here.

JEAN: I just really need you to pay attention, honey. This is nerve wracking for me.

JOE: Alright, Jean. My God, I'm barely into my second cup here.

JEAN: I know.

JOE: Alright, so just go.

JEAN: From where?

JOE: From…wherever? Where do you wana' take it from?

JEAN: Alright, let's just go from the top of the scene.

JOE: Alright. Ready?

JEAN: (*A beat, then assumes her Estelle pose.*) "*Morris, do you remember when we met?*"

JOE: (*With his usual flat delivery.*) "*What does that have to do with the price of tea in China, Estelle?*"

JEAN: "*It has everything to do with everything, Morris.*"

JOE: "*What?*"

JEAN: "*Morris, we need to remember how good things were to get us through this now. Things were so simple then. We…we….we…*" Line.

JOE: Uh…. "*We had everything before us….*"

JEAN: "*We had everything before us.*" Okay. "*Things were so simple then. We had…we had…*" Line.

JOE: "*…everything before us…*"

JEAN: Damnit. Alright. "*Things were so simple then. We had everything before us. Life seemed as if…as if…as if…*" Line!

JOE: "*Life seemed as if it were an endless horizon.*"

JEAN: "*Life seemed as if it were an endless horizon! Yes, we didn't have much money, but there was something else that took us over. We didn't live in fear.*"

JOE: "*And now we do. So what's your point, Estelle. We live in fear, Tobas, Dolores…*"

146

JEAN: Tobias.

JOE: What?

JEAN: You said Tobas again, Joe . It's To*bi*as.

JOE: Well, he wrote "Tobas" here.

JEAN: It's a typo, Joe. They're all over the place. The play-wright has glaucoma.

JOE: Alright, well, you know what the character's called, so just go with it.

JEAN: Joe, these lines are hard enough for me to learn. I at least have to hear the cue lines correctly.

JOE: The what?

JEAN: The lines before mine. If you say a name differently, it throws me.

JOE: Alright, sorry. Y'ready?

JEAN: Alright, just give me a second here. You threw me.

JOE: Let me give you the Morris line again, okay?

JEAN: Alright. Wait.

> *(JEAN takes a couple of deep and dramatic breaths, before assuming her Estelle pose, which JOE observes oddly.)*

JOE: *"So what's your point, Estelle. We live in fear.* **Tobias***, Dolores and our grandkids live in fear. The whole world's livin' in fear, Estelle."*

JEAN: *"But you can't lose sight of things, Morris. You have to have hope. You have to believe that…that…that…"* Line.

JOE: *"that God has a purpose for us…"*

JEAN: *"You have to believe that God has a purpose for us. And that means believing...believing in..."*

JOE: *"that"*.

JEAN: What?

JOE: *"believing that"*.

JEAN: *"And that means believing THAT...that..."* Line.

JOE: "we'll get through this..."

JEAN: *"And that means believing that we'll get through this. We can't lose faith."*

JOE: *"I'm not losing faith, Estelle. Tobias is losing faith."*

JEAN: *"And that's because...because..."* Damnit, line!

JOE: *"And that's because you've lost faith..."*

JEAN: *"And that's because you've lost faith!"*

JOE: *(A beat.)* *"in him."*

JEAN: What?

JOE: You didn't finish the line. *"And that's because you've lost faith in him."*

JEAN: Alright, let's go back a little. *"And that means believing that we'll get through this. We can't lose faith."*

JOE: *"I'm not losing faith, Estelle. Tobias is losing faith."*

JEAN: *"And that's because...because..."* Line!

JOE: *"And that's because you've lost faith..."*

JEAN: *"And that's because you've lost faith!"*

JOE: *(A beat, looks at her.)* *"in him."*

JEAN: *"in him!"* *(Slight pause.)* Line!

JOE: *"Don't y'see that?"*

JEAN: *"Don't y'see that?"*

JOE: *(A beat.)* Y'got more, Jean.

JEAN: *(As she begins to pace...)* Shit! Line.

JOE: *"I'll be damned..."*

JEAN: *"I'll be damned...I'll...I'll be..."* Damnit! Line!

JOE: *"if I see..."*

JEAN: *"if I see...if I see...I'll be damned if I see...if I see..."*

JOE: *"this family crumble..."*

JEAN: No, don't tell me! I'm still trying to... *"I'll be damned if I see this...if I see this family crumble..."* LINE!

JOE: *"like a house of cards".*

JEAN: Oh, Jesus Christ!!! Joe, if we can just take it from the top of the scene one more time...

JOE: *Again*, Jean? We've been through this scene 4 times since we finished our eggs, for Godsakes!

JEAN: Well, I have to get these lines, Joe. This isn't easy.

JOE: So look at the book. My God, y'got 5 weeks still. You're killin' yourself.

JEAN: I'm trying to be disciplined. Jeremy says that the sooner we're off-book, the sooner we can start establishing our characters. My God, I don't know who this woman is.

JOE: Whata' y'mean y'don't? You know her.

JEAN: Not in the way that actors need to know their characters. I need to *be* her.

JOE: She's hopeful. Like you. You know that.

JEAN: Yeah, alright, she's hopeful. But that's not a character.

JOE: Alright, she's a hopeful Jew.

JEAN: Joe, I can't play her religion. I have to make her a person, for Godsakes.

JOE: Alright, well I'm not an actor here. I'm just tryin' to help ya'.

JEAN: Honey, I appreciate it, but you running these lines with me is the biggest help. The rest of the cast has their lines almost completely memorized.

JOE: You're kiddin'.

JEAN: For amateur actors they work awfully fast, and I'm gettin' a little overwhelmed here.

JOE: It'll be fine, Jean.

JEAN: I just need to get out of looking at the script, and the more I hear these lines, the more it gets ingrained in me, okay?

JOE: Alright. So…we'll do that then. Just let me run to the bathroom, okay?

JEAN: What, your stomach?

JOE: Yeah, a little.

JEAN: It's only your 2nd cup. You usually go through 4 before you have t'go.

JOE: Yeah, I don't know. My stomach's a little nervous, I guess.

JEAN: Why? Not because of the plumber…

JOE: Jean, I just got stuff on my… Don't worry, honey. Just let me…

> *(JOE exits. JEAN picks up script, starts to murmur a few lines…)*

> *(The phone rings. She picks up…)*

JEAN: Hello? – Um, yes, but he's occupied at the moment. May I ask who…? – Yes, this is she. Who is this, please? – What? – Yes, he is currently our broker, but my husband mainly deals with… - I'm sorry? *(Pause, as she sits.)* Oh, dear God.

> *(The lights fade out and into the sounds of a newscast in progress…)*

NEWSCASTER: …*of investment broker Barry Atkinson; This arrest comes after several reports from various investors who allegedly gave large sums of their savings, 401k, and retirement annuities to Atkinson and his firm. In return, these clients received, what now appear to be, fraudulent quarterly reports documenting their investment progress. Federal agents say that they expect numerous other clients to come forward, many who still may be oblivious as to, what now appears to be, a long-standing deception by Atkinson and his firm. Atkinson had fled his home state of New York last month, and was arrested at a Nevada Spa & Resort…*

> *(The sound fades…)*

Scene 9

An exclusive light on JOE, dressed. He speaks out, as if to authorities.

A moment.

JOE: I thought why not? A little more money. So I moved it, …because I could. Mine and Jean's. I'd given him a little a few years prior…and it seemed to do well, so I thought…why not?

(Slight pause.) They said he knew his stuff. I heard only good things. I worked with people who recommended him. He became a friend, f'Godsakes... *(Slight pause.)* So I guess I'm just one a' many suckers you guys'll be talkin' to now, huh? *(Slight pause, nods shamefully...)* Jesus Christ,... I mean, I figured we'd only be working a few more years, at best,....so why not have our money double? How could that be a mistake, after what he promised? *(Slight pause.)* I mean, you work almost 30 years at a place...and it never seems like you get enough in return. What would be, after all I gave them. All my wife gave... *(Slight pause.)* Almost everything, gone. *(Slight pause.)* Jesus Christ, what we did. How we lived. For years,...my wife making us peanut butter'n jelly sandwiches, ham'n cheese... We coulda' bought lunch,...but we remembered. We both had nothing growing up. You don't forget. So...we lived these frugal lives, put our kids through college, thinking that when we stopped working, we'd be able to be a bit more liberated. Eat out when we wanted. Travel. See the world we haven't seen... *(Slight pause, restrained seething...)* Ham'n cheese,...peanut butter'n Goddamn jelly... *(Slight pause.)* And I hand our money to this man...and he uses it to by golden bathroom fixtures and vacations to Aruba... That...that sonofa... *(Slight pause.)* We'll never get it back, will we? His being in prison is supposed to be our return investment? Our interest? No. He's lived. And he has the memories of how he lived. *(Slight pause.)* Where the hell does that leave *us*?

> *(His light fades, and into a more pronounced sound of water dripping,...which soon fades into the following...)*

Scene 10

JOE sits in recliner, still, gazing out. JEAN sits in her chair, looking at him with great concern.

A moment.

JEAN: Joe? *(Pause.)* Joe...?

JOE: Jean, I just need to sit here.

JEAN: Honey,…

JOE: I just need to sit here, dear.

> *(A still moment.)*

JEAN: Joe, you haven't moved since you've come home. I'm worried.

JOE: Jean,…

JEAN: Joe, it'll be…

JOE: Jean, I just need to sit here.

JEAN: *(Slight pause.)* Listen to me.

JOE: I can't.

JEAN: Joe, I want you to…

JOE: Jean, I'm deaf, alright? I can't hear anything right now.

JEAN: *(Slight pause, gingerly…)* They said they might…

JOE: *(Hostilely rises…)* They'll do zip. By the time they get together everyone that bastard stole from,…

JEAN: Joe,…

JOE: It's done. Jesus, we're in our late 60s, for Godsakes.

JEAN: *(Rises…)* Honey,…

JOE: It means nothing, what they say they're gonna' do. It's all lip service.

JEAN: *(Slight pause.)* We can still live.

JOE: Not well.

JEAN: Not necessarily…

JOE: We can't travel.

JEAN: Why the hell can't we?

JOE: How far can we go? We still have bills to pay, property taxes...

JEAN: We have a little savings still. And we have Social Security now...

JOE: Jean, for Godsakes, it's one thing when we were working and pacing ourselves to have some comfort in our old age. But now we're there, and we don't have that, d'you understand?!

JEAN: Joe, listen...

JOE: *(Over "listen...")* We already had to shell out almost a grand to the plumber for the leak, which he couldn't fix because the problem wasn't plumbing related, so now we've gotta' pay roofers to fix our roof, and God knows what *that's* gonna' come to. What we have in savings...what I didn't hand over to that...that sonofabitch...

JEAN: Joe,...

JOE: It isn't enough, Jean. Even with Social Security. We'll be livin' like we've always lived, which means we can't... *(Slight pause.)* We're limited, Jean. Now more than ever.

(A moment, as JEAN takes this in.)

JEAN: *(With reluctance.)* What about the kids?

JOE: No.

JEAN: Joe, we can ask them for help...

JOE: Jean, it's not happening! And their help wouldn't come close to what we lost anyway. And we're not telling them anything either.

JEAN: Honey,...

JOE: No, Jean. And if the blue moon rises and they decide to call us, we ask them if *they* need anything, the same as always, y'hear me?!

(A moment.)

JEAN: So…we'll sell the house.

JOE: I'm not selling this house.

JEAN: Joe, if it isn't feasible…

JOE: We didn't work all these years to move into some cheap little senior complex where we can all wait to kick. This is our home, Jean!

JEAN: *(Pause, calmly.)* So then…let's not worry about it now. Okay? Let's just live.

JOE: We can't live the way I wanted us to…

JEAN: Honey, don't think about years from now, or even next year. My God, we don't know what can happen in a year. Anything can happen. Something wonderful could happen…

JOE: Yeah, I could die.

JEAN: Joe, don't you dare say that!!!

JOE: *(Pause, deeply.)* Jean,…I'm so sorry.

JEAN: Joe,…

JOE: Jesus, Mary'n Joseph, I thought I was being smart…

JEAN: We didn't know.

JOE: You had a trepidation. You said don't transfer so much…

JEAN: Joe, he was a friend of yours. He endeared himself to both of us. You couldn't fathom what he'd do. I questioned it just because I didn't know anything about this investment stuff. I wasn't thinking he'd turn out to be… My God.

(A moment of this realization, as JOE dejectedly sits. JEAN observes him for a moment, then resurging...)

JEAN: Now I don't want you to beat yourself up about this, Joe. It's done. We'll figure it out.

JOE: Jean,...

JEAN: And I don't want you to say things that aren't gonna' be helpful right now. We'll figure it out.

JOE: *(Slight pause, weakly.)* Will we?

JEAN: We always have.

JOE: Have we?

JEAN: Of course, we have. How in hell are we still here, for Godsakes? Over 40 years, Joe. We've been through a lot. So this is another hurdle.

JOE: Jean,...

JEAN: Okay, a *big* hurdle. So we'll jump a little higher, if we have to. Okay? *(Slight pause.)* We'll be fine.

(Car horn!)

Who can that...? *(Goes to window...)* Oh, my God, I forgot... I have rehearsal tonight.

JOE: Dr. Filbert?

JEAN: I'll just tell him I can't come tonight. It's too much...

JOE: No, Jean. Go.

JEAN: Joe, I don't want to leave you like this.

JOE: I want you to go. Go to rehearsal. I want you to. It'll be good for you.

JEAN: I don't want to...

JOE: *(Urgently rises...)* Jean, you've been with me enough. It'll be good for us. Maybe I'll... I dunno', maybe I'll clear my head and do a little brainstorming tonight.

JEAN: Are you sure...?

JOE: Yes, I'm sure. Go. Have fun.

JEAN: Have fun...?

JOE: You know what I mean. Let this be what it's been for you. It's a...it's something for you to channel stuff into. So, y'know, do that. I'm glad you have something now. Really, Jean. I want you to continue this.

JEAN: *(Slight pause.)* You're sure.

> *(JOE takes her script from the nearby end table and hands it to her, preciously...)*

JOE: I'll be fine.

> *(JEAN takes a moment before taking the script. She then takes JOE's head in her hands and gently kisses him.)*
>
> *(They look at each other with strained smiles.)*
>
> *(JEAN starts to head out, before turning to him...)*

JEAN: *(Pause.)* Everything will work out.

> *(The car horn honks again.)*
>
> *Lights out, and into...*

METEOROLOGIST'S VOICE: *Looks like we're in store for yet another pristine July day, folks. Boy, go figure Mother Nature this summer, huh? Well, no complaints here. Low humidity, light breeze coming in from the east, and temperatures currently around 65. Our high will be about 72 on the Island, and about 78 in the metropolitan area...*

Scene 11

*The sounds of early morning, as the lights come on living room.
We hear faintly the sounds of JEAN running lines, flubbing, then
repeating them again. She comes out with her dog-eared script
in hand...*

JEAN: *"Morris, he's not himself." (Looks at script, with a deep
voice.) "Then who is he supposed to be, Estelle?" (Lowers script)
"Morris, listen to me..." (Looks at script, deep voice) "Estelle,
are you trying to say it's my fault?" (Lowers script.) "I'm saying
he feels...he feels....he feels..." Shit. (Looks at script) "I'm saying he feels like enough of a failure as it is." (Lower script.) "I'm
saying he feels like enough of a failure as it is." (Looks at script,
deep voice.) "He should, the no good, two bit..." (Lowers....)
"Morris, for Heavens sake, why do you need to add to his depression? He's tried. I know he's tried..."*

JOE: *(offstage, over "tried...".)* Jean?!

JEAN: Oh. Sorry, Joe. Did I wake you?

> *(JOE enters in bathrobe, unusually energized...)*

JOE: What's goin' on?

JEAN: I was running lines. I thought I was whispering, but it's
hard to contain the emotion…

JOE: *(Over "emotion…")* That's alright. Listen, I got an idea.

JEAN: About what?

JOE: Sit down here for a second.

JEAN: Joe, what…?

JOE: Just come on. Sit.

> *(JOE sits eagerly, then JEAN...)*

So last night into this morning I've been mulling things over. About our financial situation.

JEAN: Joe,...

JOE: I'm gonna' go back to work.

JEAN: *(A beat.)* What?

JOE: At the office. Why not?

JEAN: Why not? Joe, you're retired.

JOE: Well, I can come out of retirement.

JEAN: Joe, we...

JOE: Now just wait...

JEAN: We don't need this now.

JOE: Jean, we do. I told you, in a couple of years we'll have sapped through what little savings we have, and that's just if we don't get surprised with other stuff. And we won't be able to do much with just Social Security.

JEAN: Joe, I really think we should think of something else here...

JOE: *(Rises...)* What's to think, Jean? I'll be making more money back at work. And I can set aside some money, start up another annuity for us. I'll work just a few more years. Of course I'll get vacation time too...

JEAN: *(Rises...)* Joe, I can't believe you wana' do this.

JOE: Jean, it's the best option for us.

JEAN: I don't wana' see you working if you don't want to.

JOE: Well,...let's say I do want to.

JEAN: You told me you couldn't wait to get outa' there.

JOE: Yeah, well,…that was then. Now…I'm looking at it like this was a nice little sabbatical and I'm ready to hop back on the wheel. Okay?

JEAN: I just… That's…

JOE: *(Taking her by the shoulders…)* I mean, honey, you have something to do. You have this play, right? And it's been great for you. And maybe this'll lead to other things, or inspire…you know, you to explore your artistic side. What do I have? Work. That's what I have. So it works out. We need money, I'm getting antsy sitting around doing nothing anyway, like you said, so why not?

JEAN: Well, I just… Joe,…

JOE: What?

JEAN: *(Slight pause.)* You were right, honey. For Godsakes, these *are* our Golden Years. I'm doing something exciting that I've never done before, and it scares me like hell and all that, but it's liberating.

JOE: Well, good. I'm thrilled, honey…

JEAN: *(Over "…honey…")* Honey, I'm saying we've worked all those years, and it was enough. Regardless of what was taken from us, we're entitled to just do what we want to do now, even if it's nothing. I mean, if they asked me back tomorrow, I'd tell them to go to hell.

JOE: I'm not asking you to go back to work.

JEAN: Joe,…

JOE: I don't want you to work, for Godsakes. I want you to do whatever you wana' do. I want you to live.

JEAN: And I wana' live with you.

JOE: I'm not going anywhere, honey. I'm just gonna' work again.

JEAN: I don't wana' see you go back to work because of…because of what's happened.

JOE: It's only part of the reason. Alright,…a lot of the reason, but not *all* of it. I mean, Jesus, I want us to see the world, Jean. That was the plan, right? And I do feel like going back to work. I mean, it's not bad. Like you said, they respected me there. Looked up to me. My God, Martin Kellner always said I was like a second father, for Godsakes. I mean, there are worse things to go back to. *(Slight pause.)* And I can still run lines with you before I leave in the morning.

> *(…JOE tenderly tickles JEAN's sides, as they giggle and peck.)*

JOE: Alright? So I'm gonna' call Martin on Monday. He'll be thrilled to hear from me. My God, I bet they're already fallin' behind there.

JEAN: But, honey,…

JOE: Come on, let me take us out to breakfast!

JEAN: *(Smiling…)* Oh, Joe, I can make…

JOE: No, I feel like celebrating! This is a positive thing. Right?! I'll be working at the ol' place, you'll be opening in your show soon. Hey, it's just like you said; it's worked out.

JEAN: Honey,…

JOE: Come on, baby doll, let's get dressed!

> *(He pats her butt…)*

IHOP on me!

> *(JOE excitedly exits, as JEAN looks off, cautious but smiling at JOE's ebullience.)*

> *(Lights)*

(The sounds of water dripping slightly faster and louder than before, which fade into...)

Scene 12

The sounds of a car pulling into the driveway, before the lights fade up...

JOE, similar to Scene 10, sits in chair (in shirt, tie), depressed, with JEAN sitting alongside.

A moment.

JEAN: Joe? *(Slight pause.)* Joe?

JOE: Jean, I just need to sit here.

JEAN: Honey,...

JOE: I just need to sit here, dear.

> *(A moment.)*

JEAN: Will you at least eat something? *(Slight pause.)* Joe?

JOE: *(Somewhere else.)* I go all the way down there...

JEAN: Joe,...

JOE: Coulda' told me on the phone. But they had me go all the way down there...

JEAN: Joe,...

JOE: *"Let's talk in person",* he said...

JEAN: It's just as well.

JOE: What's just as well, Jean? We needed this.

JEAN: We didn't need you working for them anymore. You gave enough.

JOE: No, apparently not. Apparently, it wasn't enough that I left when I wanted to, with my head held high.

JEAN: Joe,…

JOE: No, they wanted my humiliation too.

JEAN: Honey,…

JOE: Just like those bastards at your company.

JEAN: Joe, don't dwell on this…

JOE: *(Rises…)* You were right.

JEAN: Right about what?

JOE: God forbid you're old.

JEAN: Joe,…

JOE: God forbid a gray hair.

JEAN: Joe,…

JOE: God forbid a wrinkle.

JEAN: *(Rises…)* Honey, listen to me. They respected you. You know that. They just had to fill the position when you left. That's not unusual…

JOE: Jean, they offered me a mailroom job.

JEAN: *(Slight pause.)* What?

JOE: Martin, the one who looked up to me "like a father figure". That's what he offered, like he was doing me a favor. A former manager works for a company for over 30 years is gonna' work in a room, at half the salary, with a coupla' kids young enough to be his grandchildren. Are you kiddin' me?

JEAN: Joe, if it's all they had…

JOE: Oh, for Godsakes, they coulda' just said the position was filled and been done with it. They didn't have to demean me, and then act like they were helpin' out some poor old sap. Those Goddamn bastards, they were waiting for this.

JEAN: Waiting for what?

JOE: They were just waiting for me to come back so they could step on me like a bug.

JEAN: Joe, that's… *(A beat.)* So good riddance to them. Alright? You said "no" so it's done. We'll figure something else out.

JOE: Speakin' of bugs, I'll need to call the exterminator now.

JEAN: More waterbugs?

JOE: There's another Goddamn expense.

JEAN: I never see these things.

JOE: Well, they have nothing to say to *you*, apparently.

JEAN: When the hell do they come out?

JOE: Late at night. I've told ya'. After you go to bed.

JEAN: My God, you laid out the motels.

JOE: Not workin'.

JEAN: And the Raid.

JOE: Not workin'.

JEAN: Well, Jesus, we don't need to pay for an exterminator if they only come out late. For Godsakes, just save the money and come to bed earlier.

JOE: I'm not gonna' base my life around *them*! This is my house! It's enough we have to conform our lives because of that sonofabitch broker. Now I'm gonna' let the Goddamn bugs take over?!

JEAN: Alright, Joe, just calm down.

JOE: I am calm!

JEAN: No, you're not. Just take it easy. *(A beat.)* I guess it must be the humidity.

JOE: What humidity, Jean?! This has been the mildest summer we've had in years. We've had no rain, no humidity, and yet we have a roof leak and waterbugs!

JEAN: *(Reluctantly.)* And the basement.

JOE: *(Slight pause.)* Oh, Jesus Christ. What happened in the basement...?

JEAN: Joe, just take it easy. I went down to get the broom to scoot the raccoons from the garden and I stepped in water. There's about an inch down there.

JOE: Oh, Jesus Christ...

JEAN: It's the sump pump. We've had it forever, so I guess it was just a matter of time...

JOE: *(Over "...a matter of time...")* Jesus Christ...!

JEAN: I already called. They're gonna' come first thing in the morning.

JOE: Yeah, sure, they can come tomorrow, like the roofers have to come again next week, like the exterminator'll have to come...! This is thousands of dollars, Jean! For Godsakes, here I'm thinking we can at least get by for a little while, without traveling, and we're not even gonna' have that! At this rate, the damn raccoons'll be eatin' better than us!

JEAN: So what do we do, Joe?

JOE: I don't know, Jean!!!

(JOE takes notice that this last outburst has shaken JEAN, which restrains him and, instead sends him to an unusual place...)

(A moment.)

JOE: *(A strained attempt at comforting...)* But we'll fix it. We'll fix it. Just...keep rehearsing,...and we'll help with your lines and...I'll...I'll find something soon enough and we'll...we'll be fine.

JEAN: *(Concerned...)* Joe...

JOE: We'll be fine. I promise, honey. I'm just gonna'...look on the computer, work on a new...new résumé, and you...you look at your lines. Okay?

(As he goes off, as if in a trance...)

Just look at your lines, honey.

(...JOE slowly exits. JEAN looks off, near tears,...as the lights fade out...)

Scene 13

In darkness, we hear JEREMY as if speaking from the back of a theatre, which he does so throughout...

JEREMY (Voice): Alrighty, everyone! Now we have 2 weeks before our opening, so we should all be off book at this point and we should also be honing in on who our characters are, okay? What similarities do they have to us. What differences. What have we yet to tap into. Okay? We've done a lot of nice work these past 3 weeks. I'm seeing some really interesting things that you're all doing, but we really need to buckle down now, okay? This is the home stretch. Okay? We need to focus, we need to know our lines, some a little more than others; Jean...ahem.... And we need to get familiar with the set, now that we have it to work with, okay? Some of the paint is still a little damp, and other things are still in the early construction phase, so please be careful. Also that china cabinet has a fresh coat, so no touchy, please. Thank you very much. Alright? Now we're gonna' pick up where we had to stop last rehearsal, with the Morris/Estelle scene in Act 2/Scene 2. We're actually gonna' start at Estelle's speech, okay? Jean?

(Light comes up on JEAN, on stage...)

JEAN: Uh...yes, that's... Yes, okay.

JEREMY (Voice): Are you alright?

JEAN: I...yes, I'm...Yes, I'm...

JEREMY (Voice): Okay, very good. So we have Jean, we have Dr. Filbert, so let's take it from where we left off. *"Morris, we need to remember...*blah-blah-blah". Whenever you're ready, Jean.

(JEAN is distracted...)

Jean?

JEAN: I...yes, I'm... I'm ready.

(JEAN awkwardly assumes her Estelle-pose...)

"Morris, we need to remember how good things were to get us through this now. Things...things were so simple then. We...we...we..."

(A moment, as she attempts to recall.)

JEREMY (Voice): Just call for line if you need it, Jean, okay?

JEAN: No. I'm... *"We need... Morris,... Things were so... We...We...We..."*

JEREMY (Voice): Jean...?

JEAN: Damnit, line!

JEREMY (Voice): Jean, it's alright. Just breathe, okay? If you need a line, just say "line". I've been telling you this.

JEAN: I'm sorry.

JEREMY (Voice): Whenever anyone goes up on a line, they call "Line!". Just do the same, okay?

JEAN: Okay. Line.

JEREMY (Voice): Yes, okay. The line is *"Morris, we had everything before us. Everything seemed so simple then. Life seemed as if it were an endless horizon..."*

    (JEAN absorbs this as best she can, ...)

JEAN: *"Morris, ...we need to remember how good things were to get us through this now. Things were so simple then..."* I'm sorry, I'm a little... Sorry, Doctor. I just... Jeremy, I feel a little lost here, I think.

JEREMY (Voice): With the lines?

JEAN: Well, yes, but I think it's...it's...

JEREMY (Voice): The scene?

JEAN: The part. And I think...I think that's why maybe I'm having a hard time with the lines and the scene and the play, in general.

JEREMY (Voice): What are you not getting, Jean?

JEAN: Well, it's... Estelle, quite frankly. I guess I just don't understand her like I thought I would. I mean, she's...she's sort of the rock of this family, yes?

JEREMY (Voice): Yes, exactly.

JEAN: She...she's...y'know, she's this stabilizing force...

JEREMY (Voice): Yes.

JEAN: But...the family isn't listening to her; her son, her husband... And yet she's...she's...

JEREMY (Voice): She's still who she is.

JEAN: Well, that's the thing. Who she... What is that?

JEREMY (Voice): Whata' you mean?

JEAN: Well,...who is she?

JEREMY (Voice): Like you said, she's a stabilizing force. She's...hopeful.

JEAN: *(Slight pause.)* But...why?

JEREMY (Voice): Why?

JEAN: Why is she hopeful? I mean,...again, I'm sorry, everyone. I'm still new to this, unlike everyone else here, so...I guess...it's that old cliché of needing...needing... What is that...?

JEREMY (Voice): Motivation.

JEAN: Yes, that's... Yes, motivation. So I'm wondering what her past is, what made her marry Morris. Why is she ignoring the obvious?

JEREMY (Voice): And what's the obvious?

JEAN: *(Slight pause, almost personal.)* That...that there's no hope.

JEREMY (Voice): Well, Estelle doesn't believe that.

JEAN: Why not?

JEREMY (Voice): Well, she's...she's...she's an optimist.

JEAN: But why?

JEREMY (Voice): Why is she...?

JEAN: *(With increased aggression and emotion...)* I mean, we...we don't know anything about her. Maybe she didn't come from much herself. She *says* she didn't, but we don't know what specifically, you know? Her parents, what were *they* like? Were they encouraging? Were they...were they admonishing? We...I mean, she has to be a real person, right? I mean, she's not some...some angel, is she? She's not some stupid, idiotic symbol of...of blind faith, right? I mean, Jesus, when the house is so obviously crumbling, when her son has become a drunk, when her husband is...is getting increasingly embittered by...by every-thing. By his son, by the world... And she still believes something's going to magically happen? Something's just gonna' save this family? And pay their overdue rent and feed them...? And...and...and there's leaks, and waterbugs and...and raccoons are stealing the tomatoes and the basement is... I mean, how can you have hope? How can you have hope when there's...there's this world out there that you'll never have a chance of seeing? When you're a woman already so close to death?!!!

(JEAN is struck at her own display.)

(A moment.)

JEREMY (Voice): Um...Jean? Would you like to take a five?

(Lights out on JEAN and up on JOE with suit and brief-case in hand. He has a beaming, presentational smile...which decreases with each rejection... *Each previous Voice is repeated so that there is an endless overlap, leading to the final repetition...

Voice 1: Mr. Brancato, thank you for coming in, but we don't seem to have anything available right now. Of course we'll keep your résumé on file, should something come up...

Voice 2: *(over "right now...")* Mr. Brancato, we're not currently looking at this time, but thank you for coming in and giving us a chance to get to know you a little bit...

Voice 3: *(over "thank you for...")* No, unfortunately we don't have anything, Mr. Brancato. We've had to make some recent cuts and your salary requirements are well-beyond what we could...

Voice 4: *(over "Mr. Brancato...")* Your résumé is impressive, Mr. Brancato, but your salary requirements are a bit high for what we can afford, and frankly we think you're pretty over-qualified anyway for what we have, but we'll certainly keep you on file...

Voice 6: *(over "we can afford...")* We're very much a young, start-up company, Mr. Brancato, and we're mainly looking for college graduates just starting out...

Voice 7: *(over "looking for...")* We're not hiring, not hiring, not hiring, not hiring, not hiring, not hiring, not hiring, not hiring, not hiring, not hiring, not hiring,...

> *(All the Voices chant the "not hiring"-mantra, which continues, as the lights fade out...)*

Scene 14

JOE sits in recliner, on book for JEAN, who stands, facing out as usual. She is somewhat less animated in her performance style and has a bit more authority with her line readings now, even if still shaky...

JEAN: *"Morris, do you remember when we met?"*

JOE: *(A beat, with particularly morose-and flat- delivery.)* "What does that have to do with the price of tea in China, Estelle?"

JEAN: *"It has everything to do with everything, Morris."*

JOE: *"What?"*

JEAN: *"Morris, we need to remember how good things were to get us through this now. Things were so simple then. We had*

171

everything before us. Life seemed as if it were an endless horizon. Yes, we didn't...we didn't...we..." Line.

JOE: *(A beat, aware of the irony.)* *"We didn't have much money, ..."*

JEAN: *(A beat, aware of this, but forges on...)* *"We didn't have much money, but there was something else that took us over. We didn't live in fear."*

JOE: *"And now we do. So what's your point, Estelle. We live in fear. Tobias, Dolores and our grandkids live in fear. The whole world's livin' in fear, Estelle."*

JEAN: *"But you can't lose sight of things, Morris. You ...you ...you ..."* *(A beat.)* Line.

JOE: *(A beat, with further difficulty.)* *"You have to have hope..."*

JEAN: *(A beat.)* *"You have to have hope. You have to believe that God has a purpose for us, and that means believing we'll get through this. We can't lose faith."*

(A moment, as JOE gazes at script in hand.)

Joe? That's you.

JOE: *(Slight pause.)* *"I'm not losing faith, Estelle. Tobias is losing faith."*

JEAN: *(With some mustered confidence...)* *"And that's because you've lost faith in him. Don't y'see that? Now I'll be damned if I see this family crumble like a house of cards."*

JOE: *"It already has, Estelle. Don't y'see? The roof is cavin' in..."*

JEAN: Okay, you don't have to read all that, Joe. Can we just take it from the top of that again, just so I can get a little more comfortable?

172

JOE: Alright.

JEAN: Is that okay?

JOE: Yeah.

JEAN: And you don't have to say that whole monologue of his, Joe. You can just skip on down to my cue line and we'll go to the end of the scene, okay?

JOE: Fine.

JEAN: *(Slight pause.)* Joe,...are you sure you wana' do this?

JOE: It's fine, Jean.

JEAN: You're sure?

JOE: Yeah, I'm sure. It's...takin' my mind off things.

JEAN: *(Slight pause.)* Alright, well...good.

JOE: And y'got your dress rehearsal tonight, right?

JEAN: That's right.

JOE: Alright, so...

    (A moment.)

JEAN: God, I'm so nervous, Joe.

JOE: *(Pause, a forced grin of assurance.)* It'll be fine, honey.

JEAN: *(Pause, a forced grin of assurance.) Everything* will be fine, dear.

    (They both look at each other as if walking on emotional eggshells.)

Okay, let's take it from the top of the scene, okay?

    (She assumes Estelle pose...)

"Morris, do you remember when we met…"

(Phone Rings!)

JOE: Hold on. It might be…

(JOE urgently grabs phone…)

Yes, hello. Joe Brancato here. *(Waits, with vivid disappointment.)* Oh, hi, Doctor. - Yes, she's right here. Hold on a second.

(JOE dejectedly hands phone to JEAN.)

JEAN: Hello? – Hi, Doctor. Yes, we were just running lines. - Yes, I'm very lucky that Joe is so indulgent. - He is, yes. – Oh. Well, that's very nice of you, but… - But, I mean, it's your practice. I don't want to interfere where your patients are concer… - No, believe me, I'm aware that I could use the help, but I don't want you to feel obligated… - Well, that's very kind of you, doctor. - Yes, I know your office address. So 1 o'clock tomorrow? – Alright. And, of course, I'll see you tonight as well. – Yes, our Dress Rehearsal. Oh, my God… - Well, you're very kind. Thank you, doctor. – Alright, see you later.

(JEAN hangs up gingerly.)

Hm. How nice. He offered to meet me before our opening night tomorrow afternoon to run lines.

JOE: I see.

JEAN: He's gonna' cancel his last 4 patients.

JOE: Hm.

JEAN: He knows I'm nervous. I can't say I'm proud of that but…I can use the help.

JOE: I know.

JEAN: *(Slight pause.)* You don't feel odd about that, do you?

JOE: Odd? Why would I feel odd? You're…fellow actors, right?

JEAN: I just need all the help and confidence I can get. Oh, God, they're sold out tomorrow, Joe. Do you believe it? You're gonna' be there surrounded by these eyes that're…that're gonna' be gaping at me and I'm… I mean, Jeremy is a very good director and he's given me all these notes over the last few weeks, but I'm just…I'm overwhelmed. Dr. Filbert's done this, and I'm in most of my scenes with him so…it'll just help.

JOE: That's fine, honey. I want you to feel confident. You've put a lot of work into this, so…whatever you feel you have to do.

> *(JEAN smiles at JOE, who is still somewhere else, dark and depressed…)*

> *(A moment.)*

JEAN: Okay, so…y'wana' do this once more and then I'll make us some lunch?

JOE: *(Slight pause, flatly…)* Sure, honey.

JEAN: Joe?

JOE: *(A beat.)* I'm fine. Let's go.

> *(A moment, before JEAN assumes her Estelle-pose…*
> *JOE begins to subtly stew…)*

JEAN: *"Morris, do you remember when we met?"*

JOE: *(With slightly more intense, if still flat, delivery.)* *"What does that have to do with the price of tea in China, Estelle?"*

JEAN: *"It has everything to do with everything, Morris."*

JOE: *"WHAT?"*

JEAN: *(Taken aback as JEAN, before resuming...)* *"Morris, we need...we need to remember how good things were to get us through this now. Things were so simple then. We had everything before us. Life seemed as if it were an endless horizon. Yes, we didn't have much money, but there was something else that took us over. We didn't live in fear."*

JOE: *(A bit more intensity...)* *"And now we do. So what's your point, Estelle. We live in fear. Tobias, Dolores and our grand-kids live in fear. The whole world's livin' in fear, Estelle."*

JEAN: *"But you can't lose sight of things, Morris. You...you...you have to have hope. You have to believe that God has a purpose for us, and that means...believing we'll get through this...We can't lose faith."*

JOE: *(Unusually adamant.)* *"I'm not losing faith, Estelle! Tobias is losing faith!"*

JEAN: *(Taken aback but responding with an edge...)* *"And that's because **you've** lost faith **in him. Don't y'see that?!** Now I'll be damned if I see this family crumble like a house of cards."*

JOE: *(Rises, now clenching the script...)* *"It already HAS! Don't y'see? The roof is cavin' in! We've given everything. **Every-thing,** and what has God given us in return?!!!"*

JEAN: Joe,...?

JOE: *(Angrily and rapidly...)* *"I worked my whole damn life to raise my son only to have my son come back with his own family. Except my son is no longer here. He's gone! A figment of my memory, because that bum that spends every day at McKinley's, knockin' back Whiskey Sours is not my son, Estelle. He's a drunk! A no-good bastard who may as well a' been raised by the rats tryin' to sneak through the radiator! And I'm to feel guilty?...*

(... as JOE tosses away the script...)

*"Here I am, an old man, and I have to sell enough chestnuts to support an entire house a' six. **And what do I get?!!!** A drunk*

son, a daughter-in-law 'n 2 grandkids scared outa' their wits, and you with your high falootin' beliefs that God will save us?!!! WELL, I GOT NEWS FOR YOU, ESTELLE..." (Pause. Softly, hardly acting.) ...God...ain't savin' us."

(A still moment.)

(JEAN observes JOE, gazing out...)

JEAN: Joe?

JOE: My God, I coulda' played this part. Jesus Christ, I *am* this part! But at least this guy works, right? Yeah, he's old, but he works! *In 1929, for Godsakes!*

JEAN: Joe, calm down...

JOE: And who's playin' this part? A six-figure proctologist?!

JEAN: Joe,...

JOE: Yeah, of course; the method-acting ass doctor. The Al Pacino of the medical world... He's another one, I'll tell ya'.

JEAN: Joe,...

JOE: *(Increasingly lost in his own enraged bitterness...)* Him, all those little slicked-back executives lookin' down their noses at me. Martin Kellner, who looked up to me "like a father figure". Yeah, some Goddamn father figure...

JEAN: *(With deepening concern...)* Joe, please...

JOE: *(Over "Joe, please...")* Those snot-nose interviewers brushin'me off like I was already dead...

JEAN: Joe, I want you to listen t'me...

JOE: *(Over "I want you to listen...")* And those kids could call more often than every six months, don't ya' think? That's what we get? All those years eatin' out of a brown paper bag?!!!

JEAN: Joe, honey, I beg you, please...!!!

JOE: *(Over "please...")* The whole universe is a Goddamn conspiracy!!! THE WHOLE WORLD IS BARRY ATKINSON, THAT GODDAMN VULTURE, WAITING TO PREY ON THE ONES WHO **DARE** TO WANA' DO SOMETHIN' SPECIAL IN THEIR GODDAMN GOLDEN YEARS...!!!!!!

JEAN: JOE, STOP THIS!!!

JOE: *(Maniacal, almost threatening...)* WHAT, Y'GONNA' SAY SOMETHIN' *HOPEFUL*, ESTELLE?!!!

JEAN: *(Pause, near tears.)* I want to, Joe,...but I don't know what to say anymore.

JOE: *(Pause, suddenly choked up...)* Maybe you'd be better off with him.

JEAN: *(A beat.)* With who?

JOE: With him. The Doctor. The doctor who...who probably had everything he needed years ago, and he ain't even 60 Goddamn years old. He can offer you everything you deserve, honey...

JEAN: What the hell are you talking about...?

JOE: You can travel with him. Hell, he can take you to the Sistine Chapel. The Eiffel Tower...

JEAN: Joe, I want you to stop this...!

JOE: Where can *I* take ya', for Godsakes? The garden...?!

JEAN: Joe,...

JOE: IHOP?!

JEAN: Joe, I don't wana' hear you go on like...!

JOE: *(Over "I don't wana'...", a primal despair.)* HAM'N CHEESE, PEANUT BUTTER'N GODDAMN JELLY...!!!

(JEAN runs to JOE and grabs him by his bathrobe collar...)

JEAN: *(Over " JELLY... ")* JOE, I WANT YOU TO SHUT THE HELL UP, DO YOU HEAR ME, GODDAMNIT?!!!! *(Pause, choking back tears...)* I love you, Joe. *(Slight pause.)* We don't have to go anywhere special. We can...we can go to the beach. We can...we can...close our eyes and see the world we wanted to see,...and imagine being there. *(Slight pause, a forced grin.)* We can...we can be creative.

(JOE slowly begins to quiver and, eventually, he breaks down sobbing within JEAN's embrace, as if holding him up. Eventually, he wraps his arms around her...)

(As the lights fade, we hear a morose violin which continues for several bars before fading into an exclusive light on JEAN (as Estelle), dressed completely in black....)

Scene 15

JEAN delivers the following with a genuineness of emotion not yet exhibited in her acting...

A moment.

JEAN (as Estelle): *"For the life a' me, Morris, I don't know why he did what he did. He had everything. I know he didn't think that, with losin' his job and the Crash'n all...but he had Dolores. He had our grandchildren, Leonard and Theresa. He had us. Oh, dear God in Heaven, why couldn't...why couldn't he just see the forest for the trees? Why could he not see that, despite everything, despite how bleak everything looked, there was a light at the end of the tunnel. I believed it, Morris. I know everyone looked at me crazy when I said that, but I believed this. Maybe I was wrong. Maybe we're all fated to live hand-to-mouth for the rest of our days but, my God, Morris, let the Lord take us when he's ready. Not because we've given up. He was our son, Morris. He was our only son. (Slight Pause.) And you,...my only husband,*

Morris. So why did you have to go as well? Running down the street to save your son from himself...on that bridge, and a car...a car...strikes you. And now you're both gone. In one day. (Slight pause, choked up.) And so I'm here to look after Dolores and our grandchildren and...and I'm to believe that somehow...this is God's will? That this tragedy...is for some greater good? (Slight pause.) Well,...I honestly don't know what to believe anymore, Morris,...but I'm here. As much as I want to be with you and Tobias, I won't leave. For what remains of this family, I WON'T DARE LEAVE!!! (Slight pause, softly.) I...won't...leave."

> *(JEAN - as Estelle - looks out triumphantly, while accompanying violins, horns and thundering timpani ascend. We soon hear audience applause and, eventually, a similar light on JOE, as if in the audience, standing and clapping with emotion.)*

> *(They make eye contact from across the stage as their lights fade.)*

Scene 16

The lights fade up on the living room, as does the sounds of a distant rainstorm.

JEAN and JOE sit in their respective recliners. JEAN looking out peacefully, JOE reading paper.

A moment.

JEAN: Glad they fixed the roof in time. Huh?

JOE: *(Slight pause.)* Hm.

> *(A moment.)*

JEAN: Our first rain.

JOE: *(Slight pause.)* Yep.

JEAN: *(Slight pause.)* It's nice.

JOE: *(Slight pause, smiles.)* It is.

> *(A moment.)*

JEAN: There's a clicking sound in the car.

JOE: *(Slight pause.)* I know.

> *(A moment.)*

JEAN: It was nice having you at my opening night.

JOE: *(Slight pause.)* Sure, honey.

JEAN: And the 11 performances that followed.

JOE: Hm.

JEAN: *(Slight pause.)* I wish I coulda' comped you more than once. I know $15 a pop isn't pennies for us right now.

JOE: *(Slight pause.)* If I had to risk the roof caving in, I woulda' still seen every show, Jean.

> *(JEAN looks at JOE, a subtle grin...)*

JEAN: You really thought I was okay?

JOE: *(Slight pause.)* Jean,...you were absolutely wonderful.

> *(A moment, as they look at each other, somewhat emotionally,...before facing out.)*

> *(Eventually, JEAN looks up at ceiling.)*

> *(A moment.)*

JEAN: My God.

JOE: *(Turns to her...)* What?

JEAN: The ceiling.

JOE: *(Looks up...)* Oh, shit, is it leaking...?

JEAN: Oh, my God, Joe,...just breathtaking.

JOE: Breathtaking?

JEAN: Look, Joe. Michelangelo.

> *(JOE observes her curiously...)*

Just beautiful. *The Creation of Adam.* There it is.

> *(JOE gradually indulges, leans back in his chair,...observes the ceiling...)*

> *(A moment.)*

JOE: Rome sure gets a lot a' rain this time of year, doesn't it.

JEAN: *(Pause, smiles.)* It does.

JOE: *(Pause, with serenity...)* But y'know what? It's beautiful, just the same.

> *(A moment.)*

JEAN: Yes, it is, my dear.

> *(After a moment, they extend their hands to one another, while remaining in their momentary states of bliss,...as the lights fade...)*

End of Play

THE
DISHONORABLE
DISCHARGE
OF
PRIVATE PITTS

THE DISHONORABLE DISCHARGE
OF PRIVATE PITTS

The Dishonorable Discharge of Private Pitts received its World Premiere with fandango 4 Art House at the IATI Theatre in New York City with the following cast and production staff, November 2015:

JENNY PITTS……………………………..Brooke Turner
MRS. PITTS/ENSEMBLE…………………Judy Alvarez
MR. PITTS/ENSEMBLE…………………..Mark Ellmore
TOWNSPERSON #1/ENSEMBLE……..….John Blaylock
TOWNSPERSON #2/ENSEMBLE…Mary Ellen Toomey
CHAD/ENSEMBLE………………………Alan Hayhurst
SGT. GRAVES/ENSEMBLE…..Galen Murphy-Hoffman
MENDOZA/ENSEMBLE………………Jasmin Norwood

Directed by Kathy Gail MacGowan

Stage Manager: Bethany Clark
Lighting Designer: Michael Megliola
Sound Designer: Julian Evans
Costume Designer: Katy Freeman
Press Representative: Daniel DeMello (DDPR)
Artistic Directors: Judy Alvarez/Daniel Damiano

Special Thanks to the WorkShop Theater Company (Scott Sickles, Artistic Director) in NYC and the artists who lent their talents to previous readings:

Mary Ruth Baggot, Dan Patrick Brady, Joseph Franchini,
Richard Kent Green, Justin Herfel, Mark Hofmaier, Natalie Mosco, Jeff Paul,
Laura Piquado, Kari Swenson Riely, Laurie Schroeder, Paul Singleton,
Ben Sumrall and Jane Lincoln Taylor.

Cast of Characters

Principle Roles (in order of appearance) –

JENNY PITTS - *Ages 7 through 22, from Halibut, Texas. Small in
stature. Caucasian.*

MAN - *As Chorus, appears as TOWNIE #1 and, in Act 2, as MP #1 in
addition to multiple roles, 30's-50's.*

WOMAN - *As Chorus, appears as TOWNIE #2 and, in Act 2, as
MP#2 in addition to multiple roles, 30's-50's.*

MR. PITTS   - *Jenny's Father, early-mid 40s, burly, blue-collar, from
Texas.*

MRS. PITTS   - *Jenny's Mother, early-mid 40s, blue-collar but
feminine, from Texas.*

COUNSELOR - *Early 30's. African-American.*

CHAD   - *Group Home Resident, 17, from Texas.*

SGT. GRAVES - *US MP Staff Sergeant in Baghdad, early 40s. Burly,
Midwestern.*

PVT. MENDOZA - *US MP Private/Guard in Baghdad, from the
Bronx, NY, 26. Female. African-American/
Hispanic.*

SHERRY - *Early 20's, from Texas. African-American*

Additional Roles – Played by the Ensemble
MILITARY JUDGE, YOUNG BOY, DEFENSE SECRETARY.
PRESIDENT GEORGE W. BUSH, CHAMBERS, DELUCCI,
NEWSCASTERS, PRISON GUARDS, PHYSICIAN, CHAPLAIN

The play spans from the early 1980's through 2005, in various places.

ACT 1 - *Birth, Death, Life*
ACT 2 – *Baghdad and Beyond*

*In production, the play is intended to be performed by a cast of 8 on a
largely bare stage, with all actors but the one playing Jenny Pitts playing a
variety of roles. Specific character tracks are available with the acting ver-
sion of the play, upon request.

ACT ONE
Birth/Death/Life

An exclusive light rests on JENNY PITTS, facing out.

MILITARY JUDGE: Private, before we conclude the proceedings here today, I wanted to take this time to allow you the opportunity of speaking on your own behalf. If there is anything you feel you'd like to leave this court with, without provocation of questions or cross-examination, you may speak now.

> *(A moment, JENNY contains a wealth of emotion.)*

Have you anything you wish to say?

> *(A moment, before JENNY struggles to simply open her mouth...)*

 Private? Have you anything you'd like to say?

> *(A moment, as she attempts to speak...but cannot...)*

Jenny?

> *(A moment, before the light goes out on JENNY and up on two TOWNIES - a Man & Woman. Additional Townies, including Mr. & Mrs. Pitts, are scattered about the stage...)*

TOWNIE #1: She was pronounced dead
as soon as she was born.

TOWNIE #2: Two months premature,
three steps into death's door.

TOWNIE #1: A frail heart, they said;
How would she survive?

ALL TOWNSPEOPLE: Yet somehow she did,
"By the grace of God's Eyes."

TOWNIE #1: Her parents would say,
               to the local press,

MR & MRS. PITTS: *(Holding hands…)*
               "She was meant for this earth,
               for she is blessed."

TOWNIE #2: The "Miracle baby",
               she soon became.

TOWNIE #1: Known throughout the town,
               in which she was raised.

TOWNIE #2: A good Christian child,
               she'd soon after become;

TOWNIE #1: Creating her own prayers,
               by the age of eleven.

JENNY: *(As a hyper-energetic young girl of 11.)*
               I love God and He loves me.
               He brought me into this world
               to spread Love & Peace.
               Among all His children,
               one thing should be known;
               When you give yourself to God,
               you're never alone.

ALL: A-men!

(Lights Out on All but the TOWNIES…)

TOWNIE #2: But as the years moved on,
               things would change.

TOWNIE #1: Her behavior grew erratic;
               n' she began to stray.

TOWNIE #2: She questioned God
n'all she believed;

TOWNIE #1: fallin' in with a bad crowd,
by the age a' fifteen.

*(Lights Out and Up on JENNY, now 15,
with MR. & MRS. PITTS...)*

MR. PITTS: What the hell would prompt you to steal a Goddamn blender?!

MRS. PITTS: You make people think that you're impoverished by actin' like this.

MR. PITTS: Who put you up to this?

JENNY: Nobody. I told you...

MR. PITTS: Jenny, I can smell you lyin' a mile away. Don't you even try doin' it with me...

JENNY: I did it myself, okay...?

MR. PITTS: The clerk at the store said there were two others with ya', n'they ran off.

JENNY: They didn't tell me to'do nothin'.

MRS. PITTS: Jenny Pitts, this is a Christian house, d'you understand?

JENNY: Yeah, I...

MRS. PITTS: Lyin' is a sin.

JENNY: I'm not lyin'...

MR. PITTS: *(Over "lyin'...")* Jus' like stealin' is a sin.

JENNY: I'm not lyin', okay?

MR. PITTS: Don't waste martyrdom on somethin' like this, girl.

MRS. PITTS: Defendin' criminals is no more noble an act than stealin', you hear me?

MR. PITTS: I can tell ya' Joan of Arc didn't steal a Goddamn blender…!

MRS. PITTS: Bill…!

JENNY: No one put me up to nothin', okay? I did it myself.

MR. PITTS: Oh, so you were of your own mind. You were the brave one, is what you're sayin'.

JENNY: I did it, is what I'm sayin'.

MRS. PITTS: Why, Jenny? To prove what?

MR. PITTS: To prove that you can be even more stupid than the average teenager?

JENNY: I jus' thought it wasn't a…

MRS. PITTS: *(Over "…it wasn't a…")* You *thought*?!!

MR. PITTS: Shoot, if you actually *thought* about anything here, you wouldn't gotten busted for stealin' stuff we already have. You'd a' been in school where you shoulda' been in the first place.

MRS. PITTS: I jus' don't understand what you've become.

MR. PITTS: A Goddamn miscreant, that's what.

MRS. PITTS: Bill, alright, now don't…

MR. PITTS: *(Over "now don't…)* Shit, we work, we go to church, barely pay our mortgage n'live by the civil rules of society, while this one smokes cigarettes, snorts glue and steals appliances.

JENNY: I don't sniff no glue.

MR. PITTS: Bullshit!

MRS. PITTS: Bill,...!!!

MR. PITTS: What, she thinks I don't know? You wana' explain the missin' bottle from my workstation in the garage?

JENNY / MRS. PITTS: No... / Bill,...

MR. PITTS: *(Over "No/Bill...")* Huh? You wana' explain what I found under your bed this mornin'? You gonna' tell me you're makin' model airplanes?

MRS. PITTS: *(A beat.)* Is this true, Jenny?

MR. PITTS: Yeah, it's true. 'at's why she was 3 sheets to the wind that time she said she had too much cough medicine. She was gettin' high with 'er buddies.

JENNY: I'm not gettin' high with nobody, alright...?

MR. PITTS: *(Over "alright...?")* Then you're gettin' high by yourself, girl. n'don't you talk back t'me, y'hear...?

JENNY: n'I didn't steal nothin' from the garage...

MR. PITTS / MRS. PITTS: *(Over "I didn't steal nothin'...")*
Don't you talk back t'me, Jennifer! / JENNIFER!

   (A moment.)

MRS. PITTS: My God, you used t'be so bright.

MR. PITTS: Your mother'n I used t'read to you in the womb, for Godsakes.

MRS. PITTS: You used to write your own prayers.

MR. PITTS: n'now you can barely put two words together. What the hell sense does 'at make?

JENNY: Maybe I was adopted, okay?

MRS. PITTS: *(Slight pause.)* What?!

MR. PITTS: What the hell d'you jus' say?

JENNY: Maybe I was adopted. Alright?

MR. PITTS: *(An intense pause.)* Or maybe you just sold your soul to the devil.

MRS. PITTS: Bill, don't even...

MR. PITTS: *(Over "...don't even...")* That's the only thing that can explain you, girl, 'cause I damn sure know this ain't *our* fault.

JENNY: I didn't sell nothin'...

MR. PITTS: *(Over "nothin'...")* Now we're gonna' put an end to this right now, you hear me?! And I'll tell you somethin' else...   GET BACK HERE!

> *(JENNY stops, with her back to them.)*

Jenny,...you face me, right now.

MRS. PITTS: Jenny,...!

MR. PITTS: You turn around right...!

> *(JENNY does so.)*

MR. PITTS: *(Slight pause.)* You make one more misstep n' I will kick your butt right into juvenile hall until you're old enough t' go to prison, 'cause I'd rather have you locked away than have you keep shamin' this family.

MRS. PITTS: Bill, alright, now that's...!

MR. PITTS: *(Over "now that's...")* No, Trish. That's it! We gotta' lay down the law here. She doesn't wana' hear nothin' about our Lord and the good Christian way a' life, n'obviously nothin' we've said has put the fear a' God in her anyway...

JENNY: I don't fear God.

MRS. PITTS: You what?

MR. PITTS: *(Slight pause.)* Tell me I didn't jus' hear you say that.

JENNY: You shouldn't believe in somethin' that you fear.

MR. PITTS: God is your judge, Jennifer. Not someone you snort glue with, you hear me?

MRS. PITTS: If you don't believe that, then you don't believe in Him.

JENNY: Then I don't believe in Him, alright?

MRS. PITTS: *(Slight pause.)* Jenny,...that is unacceptable, do you understand?

MR. PITTS: Yeah, but to the blender-stealin', glue-sniffin'cult she belongs to, it's probably their damn mantra.

JENNY: I don't belong to no cult, okay...?!

MRS. PITTS: *(Over "okay...?")* Jennifer...!

JENNY: I'm of my own mind, alright...?

MR. PITTS: Yeah, well, whatever the hell you are, here's the scripture; you don't wana' fear God? That's fine. Fear me. Okay? Because as of right now, you are on borrowed time. You hear me? *(No response, with restraint.)* Jenny,...d'you hear me?

JENNY: (Slight pause, coldly.) I hear you and fear you. How's 'at?

(JENNY storms off.)

THE DISHONORABLE DISCHARGE OF PRIVATE PITTS

(A moment, before MRS PITTS takes MR. PITTS by the shoulders…)

MRS. PITTS: Let's pray for her.

(Light fade.)

(In dim light, we see Jenny and a Young Boy and another couple embracing, with the two Townies nearby…)

TOWNIE #1: From that point on,
       things'd get worse

TOWNIE #2: She'd get high,
       n'steal from her mother's purse.

TOWNIE #1: Aimlessly, she drifted
       through her wasted days.

TOWNIE #2: With so-called friends,
       living in a haze,

TOWNIE #1: a phase,

TOWNIE #2: seemingly unending,

TOWNIE #1: descending,…

TOWNIE #2: into carnality,

TOWNIE #1: with various young men,…

TOWNIE #2: void of personality.

(Light on JENNY with YOUNG BOY, alone, in an intimate embrace…

JENNY: You love me?

YOUNG BOY: Yeah, sure

JENNY: Really?

YOUNG BOY: Yeah. I wouldn't do it with ya' if I didn't. You love *me*?

JENNY: *(Slight pause, with a shy smile...)* Yeah,...I guess. Yeah. I do.

> *(They kiss and then part throughout the following...)*

TOWNIE #1: Her father would take his belt to her,

TOWNIE #2: while her mother prayed for her soul;

TOWNIE # 1: both acts, fruitless attempts,

BOTH: for abandon had taken its toll.

> *(Lights Out and Up on JENNY & MRS. PITTS in car.)*

> *(A considerable moment, as JENNY, now 16, humbled though matured slightly, occasionally looks at her mother, who looks staunchly at the road ahead. Faint sounds of 90s country music emanate from the radio...)*

JENNY: Mom?

MRS. PITTS: Yes, Jenny.

JENNY: *(A beat.)* Can we get somethin' to eat?

MRS. PITTS: *(A beat.)* Sure.

JENNY: Cattle King, maybe?

MRS. PITTS: *(A beat.)* We can pick ya' up somethin', sure.

JENNY: *(Slight pause.)* Well, can we jus'…can we jus' eat there?

MRS. PITTS: We'll get it t'go, Jenny. Okay?

JENNY: Why can't we…? *(Slight Pause.)* Mom?

MRS. PITTS: *(A beat.)* Yes, Jenny.

JENNY: I jus'… I haven't eaten anywhere outside a' that place for 6 months, so I jus' thought we could…

MRS. PITTS: *(Over "we could…")* I understand, Jenny, I'd just prefer we didn't, alright?

JENNY: But why…?

MRS. PITTS: Jenny, what's the difference. You've seen the inside of a Cattle King before…

JENNY: Can't we jus'…?

MRS. PITTS: This is a small town. D'you understand?

JENNY: *(Slight pause.)* I…whata' you mean…?

MRS. PITTS: *(Slight pause, reluctantly.)* You want eyes on you? *(No response.)* I'll run in and get you somethin' somewheres, alright? There's a place comin' up soon. Y'wana' cheeseburger?

JENNY: *(Pause. Sadly resigned.)* It's alright.

MRS. PITTS: C'mon now. Fries? A shake? *(No response.)* Jenny?

> *(A moment, as JENNY looks out window, pained. MRS. PITTS notices, turns out, as if to put on her best face.)*

MRS. PITTS: They seemed very nice there. The staff at least. At the home. Every time I came, they seemed... very warm. *(No response.)* You said the girls were nice too, right?

JENNY: *(Slight pause, with apathy.)* They were alright.

MRS. PITTS: You said they were nice when I came to visit.

JENNY: *(Slight pause.)* They were kinda' snobby. I only really became friends with one. Sherry.

MRS. PITTS: Did I meet 'er?

JENNY: *(Slight pause.)* No.

MRS. PITTS: *(Slight pause, filling air.)* She still there?

JENNY: *(Slight pause.)* She left a coupla' months before me. After she had her...

MRS. PITTS: *(Slight pause, awkwardly.)* I see. *(Slight pause.)* Well, it's nice you made a friend. Maybe you'll stay in touch.

JENNY: She's probably dead.

MRS. PITTS: What?

JENNY: *(Slight pause.)* Nothin'.

> *(A long moment, as JENNY remains gazing out window.)*

I like the name I gave 'em. William. After dad.

MRS. PITTS: *(A beat, with difficulty.)* Very nice.

JENNY: I hope he'll be alright. *(Slight pause.)* You think he'll be okay? *(No response.)* Mom, you think he'll...

MRS. PITTS: Of course.

JENNY: You do?

MRS. PITTS: Those places are designed to place children in the best possible conditions. He'll have responsible, loving parents. He'll be want for nothin'. Believe me.

(A moment.)

JENNY: *(Choked up...)* I didn't... I didn't want to...

MRS. PITTS: Jenny, please...

JENNY: I didn't wana' do this.

MRS. PITTS: We didn't have a choice.

JENNY: I had a choice.

MRS. PITTS: *(Over "choice...")* You're a minor, Jennifer. You don't get to choose somethin' like this at your age. This is a child, not a chili dog. Alright?

JENNY: *(Slight pause, weakly.)* It's not like you woulda' had to...

MRS. PITTS: Jenny,...

JENNY: Well, I...I coulda'...

MRS. PITTS: You coulda' what?

JENNY: I coulda'...

MRS. PITTS: *(Over "...coulda'...")* Coulda' raised him yourself?

197

JENNY: I…well, I'm…

MRS. PITTS: Jenny, please…

JENNY: *(Sadly, without confidence.)* Well,…I'm…I'm his mother.

MRS. PITTS: *(Slight Pause.)* Jenny, you gave birth to 'im. The people that'll raise him'll be his parents. They'll be responsible. So jus'…don't think anymore of it, alright? Please.

> *(A moment, as JENNY looks out window. MRS. PITTS turns off radio.)*

Don't think that this has been any easier for me, okay? *(Slight pause.)* This is not how it's… *(Slight pause, barely containing.)* You think I wanted to hide you out in a maternity home the last 6 months? Tellin' our friends you had pneumonia? The flu? Everything but the damned bubonic plague jus' to keep everyone at bay? Yet they still found out, because that Mexican kid who impregnated you had t'go n'brag about it.

JENNY: *(Humbly…)* He's Cuban.

MRS. PITTS: He's irresponsible, is what he is. n'if he's Cuban, he's probably a damn communist too, if he even knows the definition. You think that sonofabitch called for you once while you were gone? *(No response.)* Huh? Were you able to reach 'im yourself? *(No response.)* I didn't think so.

> *(A moment.)*

All throughout your pregnancy,…the whole time you were gone, I thought about how…how it seemed like such a blessin' when I gave birth to you, after your father'n I had tried'n tried for so long… My God, it just about killed us. *(Pause, barely containing now.)* Before you, I had three miscarriages. D'you know that?

(JENNY remains, unaware of this.)

Well,…I sure did. I was an adult. I was responsible. Your father was responsible. Everything our families weren't, n'yet it was all we could do to just conceive a living child. n'so…when you lived through dyin', we thought what more could we've asked for. It all seemed…fated. You were our little miracle, jus' like the papers said. But then…what's all *this* been, I thought? A punishment for God givin' you life? Was this some sort a' trade off? A penance? And why the hell did it have to be so easy for *you* to…? *(Slight pause, choked up.)* n'then to have t'give up…what shoulda' been my grandson, because…this jus' wasn't how it shoulda' gone. Sixteen years old… n'if we don't do somethin', it's only gonna' get worse before it gets better.

(A moment. JENNY eventually takes notice of their route…)

JENNY: You're not bringing me home?

MRS. PITTS: *(Slight pause.)* No, Jennifer. I'm not.

JENNY: Where…where are you taking me?

MRS. PITTS: We're goin' to a very nice group home in Chesterville. The agency recommended it. It's all arranged.

JENNY: It's all…whata' you mean?

MRS. PITTS: *(Over "whata' you mean…?")* This is a place that can help you. You'll get schoolin' there, n'you'll be in a controlled environment. Curfews n'all that. You'll be stronger for it. Believe me.

JENNY: *(Slight pause.)* I…I don't wana' go there.

MRS. PITTS: Jenny, please…

JENNY: *(Over "please…")* I already came from a controlled environment, mom…

MRS. PITTS: *(Over "environment…")* Jenny, trust me, it'll be fine.

JENNY: *(Near tears…)* But I been…I hadn't done anything there. I was good…

MRS. PITTS: *(Over "I was good…")* It wasn't the outside world, honey. There were rules and regulations. Your father'n I need to work, ya' understand?

JENNY: I know that…

MRS. PITTS: *(Over "that…")* We can't be over you.

JENNY: You don't have to be…

MRS. PITTS: Yes, we would. We would have to be. You can't live your life that way, n'neither can we right now. Things're too complicated.

JENNY: Whata' you mean?

MRS. PITTS: Jenny, this isn't forever. This is just what you need for now. You don't have the baby, so you can just focus on workin' on yourself, y'hear me?

JENNY: They told you I was behavin' in there.

MRS. PITTS: D'you hear what I said?

JENNY: I jus' wana' go home, mom. I jus' wana' sleep in my bed…

MRS. PITTS: *(Over "in my bed…")* Jenny, honey…

JENNY: You're givin' me away like I jus' gave away…

MRS. PITTS: Don't you say that! No one is givin' you away, Jennifer…!!!

> *(As the car nearly veers into the opposing lane…)*

> *(A breath, as Mrs. Pitts regathers…)*

My God, we've had to put what little savings we have into this place; your college money. That's the severity here, Jenny. This is for your survival that we're doin' this, especially after what you jus' went through. n'my God,…do you honestly wana' go home now?

JENNY: *(Slight pause.)* Yeah, I…

MRS. PITTS: Do you? Really?

JENNY: Well, I…I mean,…

MRS. PITTS: Why? When was the last time your father said a word to ya'? Did he come visit ya'?

JENNY: *(Pause, gazing ahead.)* He doesn't…he doesn't wana' see me.

MRS. PITTS: *(Slight pause, regretfully.)* The timing just isn't… His business has taken a dip,…n'I've had to take on some more hours at the plant, bein' I can get only so many hours at school. *(Pause.)* He's started to drink for the first time since I told 'im to stop, before you were born. You know his father was a drinker. I never thought he'd gravitate to that again,…but…he's… I'm not sayin' it's your fault, Jenny. It's jus'…how things are now. *(Pause, with deeper regret.)* I just about ripped my throat out settin' him right about the baby. You know he wanted you to have an abortion, don't you? A Christian man wanted his daughter to get a damn abortion? My Lord, that's… The man lost his faith 9

201

months ago n'it hasn't come back. n'I'm doin' all I can to hang onto mine, you hear me? And, lemme tell you, it's because I have that I'm takin' you to this place. Because I still believe that there's hope for you. *(Slight pause, choked up.)* I have to.

>*(Lights out, before an exclusive light appears on JENNY, with residents and COUNSELOR in silhouette behind her. JENNY faces out, reciting...)*

JENNY: Dear Mom,

In the 3 months I've been here, I don't really feel any closer to knowing myself or why I'm here than I did before. But I'm here because...I guess I need to be. I know that's my fault. I don't know why I got myself into the situations that I did. I just did.

I'm trying to make the most of this place. They have a decent library, so I'm reading a bit, but I feel as much of an outsider as I've felt anywhere else. What's funny is that I thought that if I were in a place where outcasts lived, I'd be accepted easier. But that's not the case. I guess it's just as well, because I really don't trust anyone here. So I'm alone, mostly, except for the group sessions.

Normally the time is taken up with them asking us what we did to get here, why we did it, what do we want to gain from being here. I don't know the answers to any of the questions. Recently though, the counselor was saying about how we should have an idea of what we want to do, sort of like a career:

COUNSELOR: Something practical that you can channel your feelings into.

JENNY: Everyone came up with things that seemed like pre-conditioned answers;

BOY #1: I wana' be a lawyer.

GIRL #1: I wana' be a doctor.

BOY #2: I wana' be a postal worker.

JENNY: Answers that seemed designed to get the counselors off their backs. Then she got to me;

>*(Throughout the following, JENNY is both within the scene and facing out…)*

COUNSELOR: What would you like to do, Jenny?

JENNY: *(Slight pause, thinks.)* I guess I like storms.

COUNSELOR: Storms?

JENNY: I was looking out the window at the time, and saw a storm cloud moving towards the building.

COUNSELOR: You want to go into Meteorology?

JENNY: Not really. More like…storm chasin'.

COUNSELOR: Storm chasing.

JENNY: Yeah.

COUNSELOR: That sounds…very dangerous, Jenny.

JENNY: I guess it is.

COUNSELOR: What…appeals to you about storms?

JENNY: I couldn't really answer. Maybe because they made noise when the sky seemed too calm. Maybe just because the storm was outside, where I wanted to be. One of the guys in the group even joked;

CHAD: *"If there was an ice cream truck outside, you'd proba-bly say you want to be the Good Humor Woman."*

JENNY: Maybe it was just the timing but, even so, for some reason,...I've come to like storms.

(Muffled thunder. The lights then change on JENNY...)

JENNY: A few weeks later, on the 4th of July, the staff orga-nized a big barbecue for the residents. I was by myself, as usual, poking at a pile of hot potato salad...when a storm cloud came over us. Everyone gathered their food and ran inside like it was the end of the world, but I stayed.

(A crash of thunder!)

(...as we see silhouettes of fleeing residents seeking refuge...)

COUNSELOR: Everybody inside! Everybody! Come on!

JENNY: I looked up at this big angry looking cloud, stood on top of the metal table...and waited for it to do its work. I thought maybe it'd strike me with lightning and either inspire me some-how...or kill me.

(She stands on chair and faces the sky, before lightning strikes!)

But it just missed. And if you want to laugh, mom,...one of the counselors actually said I must be blessed. I remember you and dad telling me that. Back then, I guess I believed it. Now I don't know what to believe. I only know that I'm in this place,...like I was in the last place. I hope I can somehow speak to you and dad soon...

(CHAD enters, a lanky, somewhat hyper young man of 17.)

CHAD: *(Over "...soon...")* Whatcha' doin'?

(Light change, as JENNY turns to him.)

JENNY: What?

CHAD: Whatcha' writin'? Journal stuff?

JENNY: *(Slight pause.)* A letter.

CHAD: They always want us t'keep a journal or somethin' in this place, so I thought...

JENNY: It's a letter, okay?

CHAD: Yeah, okay.

(JENNY faces out, as if to resume letter.)

Jenny Pitts.

JENNY: What?

CHAD: That's your name.

JENNY: Yeah, I know. Why're you sayin' it?

CHAD: I'm in your group.

JENNY: Yeah, I know.

CHAD: Chad.

JENNY: I know.

CHAD: Okay.

JENNY: You made that ice cream joke.

CHAD: Yeah, that's…

JENNY: *(Without humor.)* That was real funny.

CHAD: *(Slight pause.)* What, that piss you off?

JENNY: I didn't care one way or another. It's fine.

CHAD: It pissed you off.

JENNY: It's fine, okay?

CHAD: *(A beat.)* I saw you yesterday on the table, when the lightnin' struck.

JENNY: Alright. It didn't hit me or nothin'.

CHAD: No, I know it didn't, but it was still pretty fuckin' wild, man. The way you stood on topa' that table jus' askin' for it. Holy shit, that was audacity.

JENNY: Glad you enjoyed it. I'll be here all week.

CHAD: Seriously, man. It was great symbolism. Like somethin' outa' Greek mythology. Zeus'n all that shit.

JENNY: *(As if subconsciously.)* Joan of Arc.

CHAD: She was French.

JENNY: I know she was. I'm sayin' she did stuff like that.

CHAD: She didn't do that, did she?

JENNY: She might've. You don't know.

CHAD: Well, she was one ballsy chick, either way…

JENNY: Why are you talkin' t'me?

CHAD: Why? What's the problem?

JENNY: You haven't before.

CHAD: I dunno'. I didn't get enough of a sense of ya', I guess.

JENNY: So I stand on a table during a storm, n'now you think I'm like socially acceptable?

CHAD: Hey, it's not like I'm hoppin' on some bandwagon. Everyone else thinks you're even weirder than before, so what's the difference why I'm talkin' to ya'?

JENNY: Okay, whatever.

CHAD: Shit, you're even gettin' special treatment now 'cause they think you got some kinda' martyr complex.

JENNY: Martyr complex?

CHAD: Yeah, they didn't tell you that?

JENNY: No. Where'd you hear it?

CHAD: I didn't, but I'm thinkin' that's what they think. I been here long enough. Shit, they've given me enough fuckin' labels.

JENNY: Gee, I guess you'd be a great psychiatrist if you weren't such a fucked up resident.

CHAD: Hey, hey, hey, who says I'm fucked up?

JENNY: Who says? You're here.

CHAD: So are you?

JENNY: Yeah, n'I guess I'm fucked up.

CHAD: That what these counselors tell you?

JENNY: It's none a' your business what they tell me. That's confidential.

CHAD: Hey, fine. I'll speak for myself then, okay? I'm misunderstood. I came into this world with noble intentions and because I didn't meet the prescribed definition of adolescent normality in the eyes of my dipshit parents'n grandparents'n teachers'n guidance counselors'n therapists, I'm here. There y'go.

JENNY: You write that yourself?

CHAD: Hey, it's the truth. If I didn't believe it, I'd be like half a' these medheads here.

JENNY: So you're better than everyone else then.

CHAD: I didn't say that.

JENNY: You're not.

CHAD: I said I didn't say that. I'm sayin' you think there's somethin' defective about you, then you're settin' the table for doom, sista'.

JENNY: Okay, can I finish my letter.

CHAD: You on anything?

JENNY: What, medication?

CHAD: Yeah.

JENNY: No.

CHAD: Figured.

JENNY: Why?

CHAD: Shit, half the reason the other residents here act the same is 'cause they're all on somethin'. Irony of ironies. They all smoked and snorted everything under the sun n'now they're lo-botomized by prescription meds. *(Mock robot-like impersonation…)* *"When-I-leave- here, I-want-to-be-a-postal-worker."* Gimme a fuckin' break.

> *(JENNY barely restrains a smile, maintaining her toughened exterior…)*

JENNY: I take it you're of you're own mind, as well.

CHAD: Hell, yeah. They used t'have me on shit, until I started fakin' convulsions.

JENNY: You faked convulsions?

CHAD: Shit, yeah. I had a whole Michael Jackson thing goin' on. You kiddin'?

JENNY: Well, good for you.

> *(…as JENNY turns back out, as if to resume letter…)*

CHAD: Hell, how much you know about Joan of Arc anyway?

JENNY: What?

CHAD: That she was a rebel, n'that's it?

JENNY: I know some, okay…?

CHAD: Okay, but you think everyone didn't think she was fucked up? A practically pre-pubescent chick says she hears the "voice of God" tellin' her to lead an Army? HE-LLO!!! Even the French thought she was nuts, but, hell, those needle dicks weren't gonna' take charge, so sure, they said, we'll let the little girl represent our entire flippin' country. n'fuck if she did. Now all anyone knows is 'at she's the hero of all motherfuckin' heroes.

JENNY: *(Slight pause.)* Yeah,…alright. So?

CHAD: I'm jus' sayin, if you think you're jus' another one a' these lost souls, fine. But I'll tell ya' somethin', I ain't never seen anyone dare to be struck by lightnin' like that. That can mean you're exceptional or an exceptional fuck-up,…but that's your call, I guess.

(A moment. JENNY momentarily taken aback by this.)

JENNY: Who's to say I wasn't jus' tryin' to kill myself?

CHAD: *(Slight pause.)* Were you?

JENNY: *(Slight pause, defensively turns back out.)* It's jus' somethin' I did, okay? It wasn't heroic or nothin'. It was jus' somethin' I did. I don't' know why. I'm sure you've done all sorts of stupid stuff.

CHAD: Depends what you think of as "stupid".

JENNY: Oh, that's right. 'cause you're "misunderstood".

CHAD: Hey, I tried to off myself once. Wouldn'ta' been the way you tried.

JENNY: *(Sharply.)* I didn't say I tried to kill myself!

CHAD: I didn't say you tried.

JENNY: Well, I didn't.

CHAD: Well, good for you, Storm Chasin' Jenny Pitts.

JENNY: *(Slight pause, simmering down.)* Can't imagine some-one as smug as you would try it.

CHAD: You think I'm smug?

JENNY: Are you serious?

CHAD: I'm not smug. I'm just…confident.

JENNY: Shit.

CHAD: You really think that?

JENNY: What's it matter what I think?

CHAD: You don't think I'm funny?

JENNY: *(Slight pause.)* The Good Humor line was funny.

CHAD: You didn't laugh.

JENNY: I did later, in my room. But I didn't appreciate it at the time.

CHAD: Well, you know what they say.

JENNY: What?

CHAD: *(Smiles.)* Laughter is the best Prozac.

(Light change, as JENNY faces out…)

JENNY: Dear Mom & Dad,

Sorry I'm writing so much, but I just want to keep in touch. It's only the day after my last letter so I don't really have anything new to tell you except that…today I had Oatmeal for breakfast and a Turkey Club for lunch. And I started to talk to someone. And I miss you both.

(Light change, JENNY and CHAD laughing, later that day…)

CHAD: What, I was jus' bein' honest.

JENNY: I still can't believe you did that.

CHAD: Hey, she wanted to know what I'd do to make the world a better place, so I told 'er.

JENNY: Yeah, but you told her while doin' some Miss America impression.

CHAD: That's my point. It's a stupid question to ask anyone, let alone those ditzy bitches. I mean, they don't really care what we say here anyway. *(like a ditzy contestant)* *"I'd Have Everyone Love Each Other"*, *"I'd have everyone say 'Hi'!"* Bullshit.

JENNY: At least you didn't give *me* shit this time.

CHAD: 'cause what you said made some fuckin' sense. You'd make people stand up for what they believe in. That's cool.

JENNY: Yeah, …'cept I don't know myself.

CHAD: Ah, c'mon, St. Joan. You don't know? You mean to tell me you ain't never heard the "Voice of God"?

JENNY: I don't believe in 'im.

CHAD: Well, shit, welcome to the 90s.

JENNY: You neither?

CHAD: No one's given me a good reason, as yet. But then, I think you can do great things and believe in nothin' more than an ingrown hair. That's why things'd be easier if we were heroes, y'know?

JENNY: Whata' y'mean?

CHAD: 'cause when you're a hero, no one questions ya'. They jus' shut up. *"Too bad there ain't no war"*, as they say.

JENNY: Who says that?

CHAD: My grandfather. After my prick father gave up on me ever becomin' a cop like him, he shipped me off t'live with my grandparents, who just about had synchronized strokes before they dumped me in here. n' anytime my grandfather disapproved of stuff I was doin, he'd always say shit like *"In my day, men were men. They fought for their country."* That's probably why my father became a cop'n beat the shit outa' my mother; too young for one war, n' too old for the other. So he creates his own. Like that's what's definin' him as a man, insteada' some limp-wristed pansy-ass.

JENNY: That's what he thinks you are?

CHAD: *(Slight pause, offguard.)* Well, well, well. I guess you'd be a great psychiatrist if you weren't such a fucked up resident. *(A beat, then a weak snicker.)* Yeah, somethin' like that.

> *(An odd moment, as CHAD looks out. JENNY picks up on this…)*

JENNY: Hey,…my grandfather was kinda' fucked up too. My father's father. Big fat drunk. *(Slight pause.)* My father wasn't even speakin' to 'im when he died.

CHAD: 'Cause a' that?

JENNY: *(Slight pause.)* I dunno'. Probably 'cause…he didn't wana' be like him.

CHAD: Is he?

JENNY: *(Slight pause.)* Kinda'. Thanks t'me, I guess.

(CHAD picks up on this…)

(A moment, before CHAD hops up…)

CHAD: *(Regathering his usual self.)* Anyway,…I got some ideas.

JENNY: About what?

CHAD: Things I can do while I'm here to *"make the world a better place."* Be part a' the solution insteada' the problem.

JENNY: Like what?

CHAD: *(A smile.)* Well, that's confidential.

JENNY: Fine. See if I care.

CHAD: You don't wana' know?

JENNY: I jus' said I did, but I ain't gonna' beg.

CHAD: Fine.

JENNY: Hell, I may have a better idea than you anyway.

CHAD: Like what?

JENNY: *(A smile.)* Well, that's confidential.

CHAD: Alright, very funny. Hell, I'm surprised you haven't done anything yet anyway.

JENNY: Like what?

CHAD: Come on, you challenge Mama Nature to fry your ass and you tell me that you've never done somethin' heroic?

JENNY: What the hell could I do? I'm only 16.

CHAD: Hey, Joan of Arc was 12.

> *(JENNY is taken aback by this, and ponders, regret-fully...)*

JENNY: I stole a blender once.

CHAD: *(A grin.)* You need it?

JENNY: *(A grin.)* Tsch. Who needs a blender?

CHAD: I dunno'. Maragaritas?

> *(CHAD starts laughing, as JENNY joins in...)*

Shit, if that's heroic, I must be fuckin' Superman. Holy shit...

> *(They continue to laugh together, ...as their Light fades out.)*

> *(In dim light, residents are dispersing under the follow-ing announcement - as if via intercom...)*

COUNSELOR : *Boys and girls, dinner hour is officially over. If you are still in the cafeteria or lounge area, please report to your rooms. Once again, dinner hour is officially over. If you are still in the cafeteria or lounge area, please report to your rooms.*

Inspections will begin promptly. Thank you and have a good evening.

> *(Lights Up on JENNY with a small plastic bag, which she presents to a waiting CHAD. They speak in hushed tones...)*

JENNY: Check it out.

CHAD: Man, you weren't fuckin' around.

JENNY: You know it.

CHAD: *(Looking in bag...)* Shit, girl, you got more than me.

JENNY: 'Course, what the hell you expect? It was my idea.

CHAD: Whata' we do with 'em?

JENNY: Well, shit, we're not gonna' knock 'em back with a glassa' Kool Aid. I dunno, flush 'em down the toilet?

CHAD: Sounds like a plan.

> *(They high-five...)*

JENNY: See ya' at breakfast?

CHAD: Yeah, I'll see ya' down there.

> *(They begin to part...)*

JENNY: Hey, Chad!

CHAD: What's up?

JENNY: You're sure they don't have surveillance cameras around here?

THE DISHONORABLE DISCHARGE OF PRIVATE PITTS

(A brief alarm!)

(Light change on JENNY with COUNSELOR.)

COUNSELOR: Jenny?

JENNY: *(Slight pause.)* Yes?

COUNSELOR: How are you?

JENNY: *(Slight pause.)* Okay.

COUNSELOR: We're concerned, Jenny.

JENNY: About what?

COUNSELOR: Jenny, we know that it was a very difficult transition for you to come here, okay? I've been here long enough. I've seen all the residents go through it, in one way or another.

JENNY: Okay.

COUNSELOR: But I'm afraid we're not seeing the progress that we'd hoped to see from you. Okay?

JENNY: Whata' y'mean?

COUNSELOR: I think you're closing yourself off, Jenny, and I think this has been enhanced by who you're surrounding yourself with.

JENNY: Whata' y'mean?

COUNSELOR: Jenny, you know I'm talking about Chad. He's the only one you speak to.

JENNY: Well, what's wrong with me speakin' to him?

COUNSELOR: *(Slight pause.)* Chad is a danger to himself, Jenny. And in being so, we feel he's a danger to you.

JENNY: He's not...

COUNSELOR: I know you consider him a friend, but I just think you should try to be social with others. Others who're...less resistant to things here. Okay?

JENNY: But that's...

COUNSELOR: Chad doesn't like it here, Jenny.

JENNY: Yeah, I know.

COUNSELOR: And we feel he's encouraging you to feel the same.

JENNY: He's not. I already felt that way.

COUNSELOR: But he's influencing you. Do you see what I'm saying?

JENNY: But he's not...

COUNSELOR: Jenny,...

JENNY: That's not true.

COUNSELOR: Then you're influencing each other, and not in a good way. Alright? Now listen to me here, okay?

JENNY: What?

COUNSELOR: You two hang out together.

JENNY: *(A beat.)* Yeah.

COUNSELOR: Are you secretly…?

JENNY: *(Slight pause.)* What?

COUNSELOR: You can tell me.

JENNY: Tell you what?

COUNSELOR: Jenny, are you and Chad dating?

JENNY: How can we date?   We can't even leave here without supervision…

COUNSELOR: Jenny,…

JENNY: We're not.

COUNSELOR: 'cause residents cannot be romantically involved here, y'know.

JENNY: We're not. I don't like him that way. We're just friends.

COUNSELOR: Just friends.

JENNY: We just talk about stuff.

COUNSELOR: You laugh at the same things.

JENNY: Yeah.

COUNSELOR: Like how stupid every else is here? How stupid the world is? How no one understands you?

JENNY: *(Slight pause.)* Kinda'.

COUNSELOR: And I guess you also share the same sense of rebellion. Like stealing medications from some of the other residents?

JENNY: *(Slight pause.)* It was only from a few...

COUNSELOR: Jenny,...

JENNY: We didn't use 'em...

COUNSELOR: Okay, but...

JENNY: We were tryin' help 'em...!

COUNSELOR: Oh, I know. As Chad told me, you were trying to *"liberate the residents to be free thinkers."* Right?

JENNY: Yeah,...

COUNSELOR: And this was Chad's idea, right?

JENNY: No, it was mine.

COUNSELOR: *(Slight pause.)* Yours.

JENNY: Yeah. We were talkin' about ways to get people to open their minds without being lobotomized'n stuff, so I...suggested stealin' their meds from their rooms.

COUNSELOR: And Chad agreed.

JENNY: *(Slight pause.)* Yeah.

COUNSELOR: *(Slight pause.)* And would *you* agree with Dennis Barker having a seizure as a result of his absent medication?

JENNY: He had a seizure?

COUNSELOR: *(A beat.)* No,...but he could've. The point I'm making, Jenny, is that Dennis didn't come here to have his life put in jeopardy. His parents have him here for a reason, just like your parents do. Except Dennis has shown a desire to get something out of this. He now wants to have a responsible life; a career as a postal worker. You want to judge him because of that then that's something for *you* to get over, not him. Do you understand?

JENNY: *(Slight pause, ashamed.)* Mhm.

COUNSELOR: There's no nobility in forcing your under-developed philosophies on others, Jenny. How far you go in this life is dependent on finding out what *your* place is in the world. Who *you* are, what *you* can contribute positively. Just like we talk about in group. Okay?

JENNY: *(Slight pause.)* Okay.

COUNSELOR: Good. *(A beat.)* So that said, we're putting Chad on a different floor.

JENNY: What....I'm... Why...?

COUNSELOR: Jenny,...

JENNY: You don't need t'do that, alright...?

COUNSELOR: *(Over "...alright...?")* Jenny, we feel it would be best if you distance yourself from him for the duration of the time that he's here, okay...?

JENNY: You're just separating us...?

COUNSELOR: He'll be of age to leave on his own soon and, if you continue alienating everybody else, that's gonna' leave you by yourself again, without any friends. How will you feel then? And any sort of massive change can leave you in a profound state of despair, and we don't want to see you go through that again. That's how you came here. Remember? After you gave up your...

JENNY: *(With sudden emotion...)* I remember!

(A moment.)

COUNSELOR: Okay, sweetie?

JENNY: *(Slight pause.)* Chad's the only reason I can tolerate this place.

COUNSELOR: It doesn't have to be that way.

JENNY: Well, it *is* that way, okay...?!

COUNSELOR: Jenny,...

JENNY: *(Panicked...)* When I was at that maternity home, I had one girl who I trusted. Okay? Sherry. She was the only one who I felt wasn't fulla' shit, n'as soon as she had 'er baby, they tossed her. She didn't wana' go, but she had to, okay? And now she's probably dead.

COUNSELOR: Why d'you think that?

JENNY: 'cause she didn't have any place t'go! She told me!

COUNSELOR: Well, Jenny,...Sherry's fate doesn't have t'be Chad's. He does have family.

JENNY: But they don't want him...

COUNSELOR: *(Over "...want him...")* Jenny, Chad is not your responsibility. You have parents, and you have people here, such as myself, who have your best interest at heart. Chad is not one of 'em. And you shouldn't feel responsible for him.

JENNY: *(Slight pause.)* Have you talked to my parents?

COUNSELOR: We've had to tell them about the pill incident, but this is confidential. Between us.

JENNY: I don't care about that. They haven't talked t'*me*. Jus' a coupla' letters from my mother.

COUNSELOR: Well, we do recommend that they keep a distance in your first few months, Jenny. We've told you that. *(Slight pause.)* I will have to tell them if you're unwilling to work with the program here, Jenny, because it won't do you any good being here…

JENNY: Then jus' let me go home.

COUNSELOR: Jenny, you know that's not the answer…

JENNY: Well, what…? I mean, I…I…

COUNSELOR: Jenny,…

JENNY: I don't wana' be forced to be friends with people!

COUNSELOR: Jenny, everyone has been through similar experiences…

JENNY: *(Over "similar experiences…", desperately…)* I don't care! It…it doesn't mean we're all the same. I shouldn't even be here in the first place…!!!

COUNSELOR: Where should you be, Jenny?!

(Jenny is still, uncertain…)

Jenny, you're here because…

JENNY: *(Over "…because…")* I know why I'm here, alright?

COUNSELOR: Jenny,...

JENNY: *(Grasping...)* Look if...Chad doesn't have me, he doesn't have anybody, okay? His family hates 'im, his girlfriend dumped 'im,...

COUNSELOR: *(Over "dumped 'im...")* Jenny, listen t'me...

JENNY: He's been suicidal before...!

COUNSELOR: And so have you!

JENNY: *(A beat.)* I...I...

COUNSELOR: What was that display during the storm? For your career?

JENNY: *(Slight pause, barely masking her shame.)* That...that wasn't because of him. We weren't even talkin'...

COUNSELOR: *(Over "...talkin'...")* I know that, Jenny. But what was it because of? *(Slight pause.)* It's because you have your own issues to deal with. *(No response.)* Jenny, as much as it pains me to say it,...Chad is who he is; a lost soul. Is that who you wana' be?

> *(A moment, before the lights fade into an exclusive light on JENNY, reciting... A silhouette of Mr. & Mrs. Pitts in the distance...)*

JENNY: Dear Mom & Dad,

I've been having these dreams a lot lately. I haven't known what to make of them, really. It's like I'm on a small tugboat or something...and I'm out in the middle of an ocean somewhere. I can see this image in the distance, but it's getting closer each night, each time I have this dream. Then last night I got close enough to make out what it is; it's the two of you.

(A dim light on a still Mr. & Mrs. Pitts.)

I can see your faces, but you aren't moving. Then the boat starts to pull away from you. I call out to you, but you won't look at me. I scream but you won't so much as move. It's like…you're statues.

(Lights fade on dream imagery…)

Then I wake up. Alone. And you're not here. No one is. And the one friend I've made,…they won't let me be friends with anymore. I've been giving the counselors notes to give him, but I don't know if he's getting them. *(Slight pause.)* His name is Chad.

(JENNY's Light dims and appears on CHAD reciting a journal entry, …)

CHAD: As I write this entry, it is my 18th birthday. I don't bare any ill will for Jenny not dropping me a note. I know it's not her doing. I know the set up here is not conducive to humanity. They think they're so modern here, but all they really want is us to be their idea of what "cured" is, but we can't be cured of anything. They don't know what to cure us of. I mean, sure, some kids are pretty fucked up here, as Jenny said once, but they don't need a cure. They need a world that won't let them feel the need to be in a place like this; Quarantined. I don't need to feel that,…but I do. I guess I've felt that way all of my life. *(Slight pause.)* I think I'm gay…and, leaving here, I don't think that'll make the road any easier for me,…because there's no cure.

(He steps onto chair, as he looks at JENNY…)

Jenny,…whatever you got that gives you the courage to stare a storm in the face and spit in its eye, don't let them cure you of it. Be who you are,…even if it kills you.

(CHAD remains atop chair, as the TOWNIES appear in dim light…)

TOWNIE #1: With those parting words,
              his last entry was made,

TOWNIE #2: in a journal filled with aspirations
              he seemed to know would fade.

TOWNIE #1: As he stood upon a chair,
              void of innocence from birth,

TOWNIE #2: he wrapped a sheet around his neck,
              and soon would leave this earth.

(CHAD drops off chair into a sudden black out, before an exclusive light appears on the now sobbing JENNY…)

JENNY: Mom, Dad…please take me home!

(Her light fades into the sounds of a distant rainstorm…)

(As the lights fade up, we see JENNY sitting by a window in her room, seemingly catatonic. She remains immobile.)

(A moment, before MR. PITTS enters with a pill in hand. He has become somewhat frail over time, collectively from drink, guilt & depression, which he is just coming out of.)

(He observes her, regretfully, for a moment…)

MR. PITTS: Jenny? *(No response.)* Jenny, I've got your pill here. Y'wana…?

> *(As if on reflex, JENNY holds out her hands, while remaining in her state. MR. PITTS gives her pill, then water. A moment.)*

You should eat somethin'. Y'wana' sandwich?

> *(JENNY remains still.)*

Y'gotta' eat somethin', Jenny. Y'can't jus' take these pills. Doctor said you gotta' have food in ya', okay? *(No response, then a forced smile.)* Peanut butter'n banana sound good? I know way back when you used t'really… *(No response.)* Well, your mom'll be home from work soon. She'll…figure somethin' that you like, okay?

> *(A moment, before MR. PITTS timidly takes glass from JENNY, motions to leave. Then stops.)*

It's…it's good to have ya' back home. We're…we're really glad you're here. *(Slight pause.)* n'…n'I don't want you to think that…I ever forgot about ya'. Okay? *(Slight pause.)* I guess… I jus'… I felt for a while like you…got away from us. I haven't known…what t'make of ya'. I mean, I thought we did everything we could,…but I guess… *(Slight pause.)* Bein' force fed Christ probably didn't help. Maybe you jus' had to…figure things out for yourself and you're still searchin'. I jus' never questioned things when I was your age, so it's…it's been… kinda' tough for me, y'know? Now I'm questionin' things myself. Maybe that's good, …but your mom sure ain't happy about it. *(Slight pause.)* Right now, I'd jus' like you t'be able to smile or…somethin'. Shoot, I feel like I haven't seen your teeth since you were yay high. But I guess this is somethin' we jus' gotta'…work through as best we can. So…I jus' want you t'know that…your mom'n I'll be here for ya', okay? We won't send ya' anywhere else. We'll jus'… Alright?

(JENNY remains immobile, as MR. PITTS awkwardly observes her, before motioning to leave…)

JENNY: *(Still gazing out, as if these are her first words in some time.)* Dad?

MR. PITTS: *(Taken aback…)* Ye…yes, honey?

JENNY: *(Slight pause.)* Why didn't I stay dead?

MR. PITTS: *(Slight pause.)* What?

JENNY: *(Slight pause.)* Don't most things that die…stay dead?

MR. PITTS: *(Slight pause.)* I'm…not sure what you're askin'.

JENNY: *(Slight pause.)* Why did I live? Why…why'm I here?

MR. PITTS: *(Pause, then grasping…)* Jenny, you're… God…has a plan for…everyone.

JENNY: I thought you didn't believe in God anymore.

MR. PITTS: *(Pause.)* I…I don't know why we're here, Jenny. Why you survived was…a miracle. What you've lived through up 'til now's been…unfortunate…but…life is… Things can change. We… You can find out… I mean,… You'll find a purpose for yourself. You'll…we'll get through this. Okay? *(Slight pause, a forced smile.)* Grilled cheese sound good?

JENNY: Get through what?

MR. PITTS: T'mato soup…?

JENNY: Get through what, dad?

MR. PITTS: *(A beat, reluctantly.)* What, Jenny?

JENNY: Get through life? *(Slight pause.)* How am I gonna' do that, dad?

MR. PITTS: *(Pause, grasping...)* Jenny, when...when you're born,...you... You jus' wouldn'ta come into this world if there was nothin' for ya'. I mean, sure, there are a lot of wastes of space out there, but...that can't be you. It just... *(Slight pause.)* Your mother'n I...we wanted nothin' more than to have a family, for the longest damn time. Just one child. That's all I wanted. And you were it. I didn't...y'know, I didn't expect greatness. I didn't even expect a girl. Shoot, maybe...if you were boy, I'd have more to say here. Shit... *(Slight pause.)* I jus' expected happiness. A normal happy family. When I tell you, you were...my reason for everything, Jenny.... Even before you got here. Everything I worked for, n'everything I'm still tryin' t'... *(Slight pause.)* I know it looks dark with all that's gone on with ya' but...I'm tellin' ya', there's a light...or somethin'. If it's God or whatever the hell, I dunno', but there's somethin'. Somethin' that'll come along and...I dunno', but... I...I jus'... Jenny,... *(Slight pause, emotionally.)* Jenny, I... Your dad's only been sober a few weeks now, so...I don't know if I'm sober enough t'make sense to ya'. Maybe...maybe you should bring this up with your therapist...

JENNY: *(Suddenly.)* No, dad. You talk t'me. Even if it's shit,... YOU TALK T'ME!

(A moment. MR. PITTS remains still, shaken.)

MR. PITTS: All...all else I can say, Jenny, is that...you were born,...you died,...but...you survived. *(Slight pause.)* You're here, Jenny.

(In dim light, we see a gathering of Townspeople in two groups...)

TOWNSPEOPLE #1: You're here, Jenny.

TOWNSPEOPLE #2: You're here, Jenny.

ALL but JENNY: You're here.

JENNY: *(A beat, hopelessly, facing out.)* Why?

(A beat.)

TOWNIE #2: And then…

TOWNIE #1: …one day.

> *(TOWNIE # 1 & 2, having stepped forward from the crowd, each extend their arms, simulating planes. The sounds of large plane engines are heard, which build into a thunderous crash.)*

> *(The Lights slowly dim, replaced by the sounds of mass hysteria and sirens…)*

> *(*The ensemble form as Newscasters, which JENNY observes as if watching the events firsthand. The newscasts – below - are recited once in full volume before continuing under the subsequent newscasts in a loop, which, after several lines, are ultimately all overlapped by the President's speech - below.)*

NEWCASTER 1: We have just received word that a Los Angeles-bound plane, American Airlines Flight 11, which departed from Logan Airport in Boston this morning, has just crashed into the North Tower of the World Trade Center in downtown New York City at 8:46 this morning. *(…repeats under the following…)*

NEWSCASTER 2: At this time, we can only presume that this was accidental, though it is unusual considering the exceptionally clear skies today. Therefore, we can only attest that visibility could certainly have not been an issue. On board are said to be

76 passengers and a crew of 11… *(…repeats under the follow-ing…)*

NEWCASTER 3: *(begin at "On board are said to be…")* It has just been brought to our attention that a second plane, United Airlines Flight 175, which also departed from Logan Airport in Boston containing 51 passengers and crew of 9, has crashed into the South Tower of the World Trade Center at 9:03 this morning…. *(…repeats under the following…)*

NEWSCASTER 4: *(begin at "World Trade Center…")* This confirms the earlier though remote suspicion that the initial crash in the North Tower may have been intentional. And now, much to the city and World's great fear, it appears that these were indeed highjacked planes that have been deliberately flown into these buildings… *(…repeats under the following…)*

NEWSCASTER 5: *(begin at "deliberately flown…")* American Airlines Flight 77, which departed from Dulles International Airport at 8:42 this morning en route to Los Angeles containing 53 passengers and a crew of 6, has apparently been high-jacked and crashed into the Pentagon as of 9:37 this morning. This follows the earlier attacks on the World Trade Center, in which 2 other Los Angeles-bound planes were flown directly into the North and South Tower… *(…repeats under the following…)*

NEWSCASTER 6": *(begin at "2 other Los Angeles-bound…")* We have a just received word that United Airlines Flight 93, which departed Newark International Airport at 8:42am en route to San Francisco, has crashed in an open field near Shanksville, Pennsylvania at 10:03 this morning. Due to the horrific earlier events of the day, it is concluded that indeed this was likely to be a 4th high jacked plane. However, it appears that this one did not make it to its intended target, which authorities are saying could possibly have been the White House…

(As the Newscast loops continue in hushed tones, the PRESIDENT emerges. He speaks with unusual

authority, which ascends in intensity…)

PRESIDENT BUSH: "My fellow Americans, on September the 11th, enemies of freedom committed an act of war against our country. The evidence we have gathered all points to a collection of loosely affiliated terrorist organizations known as al-Qaida. This group and its leader, a person named Osama bin Laden, are linked to many other organizations in different countries. We have seen their kind before. They're the heirs of all the murderous ideologies of the 20th century. By sacrificing human life to serve their radical visions, by abandoning every value except the will to power, they follow in the path of fascism, Nazism and totalitarianism. AND THEY WILL FOLLOW THAT PATH ALL THE WAY TO WHERE IT ENDS IN HISTORY'S UN-MARKED GRAVE OF DISCARDED LIES!!!"

(SILENCE.)

(The PRESIDENT turns to face JENNY, who now stands before him…)

"The hour is coming when America will act,…and *you* will make us proud."

(A massive explosion, as if from a landmine.)

(Lights)

End of Act 1

ACT TWO
Baghdad and Beyond

A light appears on two MPs (Man & Woman) standing at attention, while a silhouette of soldiers, including JENNY, go into various training poses throughout:

MP #1: Not long after the attacks,
        Jenny would become inspired.

MP#2: She enlisted in the US Army,
        as if to raise herself from the mire.

MP#1: She worked harder than any soldier,
        mastering tactics of all kind,

MP #2: before transferring to a Baghdad prison,
        where she was now assigned.

    (The MPs each pivot out and march off opposite sides of the stage. An explosion occurs as the Lights come up to reveal JENNY, 20, at attention, before SGT. GRAVES.)

GRAVES: So you're our newbie, huh?

JENNY: Yes, Sergeant!

GRAVES: Do you understand what you're here to do?

JENNY: Yes, Sergeant!

GRAVES: And what is that?

JENNY: Serve and protect my country to the very best of my ability, while upholding the standards of moral integrity, courage & valor that are the vital components of the United States Army!

GRAVES: *(Slight pause, a chuckle.)* Well, shit. You write that yourself, Private?

JENNY: Yes, Sergeant. I did.

GRAVES: You believe it?

JENNY: Yes, Sergeant.

GRAVES: *(Slight pause.)* Stand easy.

(JENNY does so. A moment.)

Daughter of a veteran, by chance?

JENNY: No, Sergeant.

GRAVES: Really.

JENNY: Yes, Sergeant.

GRAVES: What's your dad do?

JENNY: He has his own air conditioning repair business, Sergeant.

GRAVES: Successful?

JENNY: Not of late, Sergeant.

GRAVES: Sorry to hear that. Your mother?

JENNY: She teaches kindergarten and works part-time at a chicken processing plant, Sergeant.

GRAVES: Well, there's a blend of occupations for ya'.

JENNY: Yes, Sergeant.

GRAVES: Only child?

JENNY: Yes, Sergeant.

GRAVES: *(Slight pause.)* Got an older brother myself. Father served in 'nam. Brother lost an arm'n a leg during the Persian Gulf War, while I was a prison guard back in the states. Now my brother's hoppin' around like a friggin' pogo stick tryin' t'get a job jus' to pay alimony to his ex-wife'n kids, and I'm here; inspired by his sacrifice. So you figure, well, veteran background, worked in a prison, passionate about the U.S. of A, of course he's here, runnin' a prison with that type of experience. Who else would you expect? Right, Private?

JENNY: Yes, Sergeant.

GRAVES: Yet here you are. Here purely by your own ingrained passion to serve and protect. But, apparently, it wasn't enough to just…go to college or get your GED and go to a police academy in your hometown. No. You had to enlist. *(Slight pause.)* You got yourself conditioned pretty well, I'll say that.

JENNY: Sergeant?

GRAVES: Sayin' all the right things, which of course we all believe here. There's no denying that our presence here is an extension of who we are; proud Americans. And this is a noble thing you're doin', Private. You've gotten yourself in shape, you're a good shot, I hear. But that nobility and training is not in and of itself gonna' coast you through your duties here, y'understand?

JENNY: Yes, Sergeant.

GRAVES: We are guarding a prison populated by some of the most heinous manifestations that have ever crawled into this sandy world.

JENNY: Yes, Sergeant.

GRAVES: We've seen what they've done.

JENNY: Yes, Sergeant.

GRAVES: On our own soil, for Godsakes.

JENNY: Yes, Sergeant.

GRAVES: And here they are, all around us. This is one dangerous place you've come to, Private. This ain't Six Flags, okay?

JENNY: Yes, Sergeant.

(SGT. GRAVES paces a bit, looks her over.)

GRAVES: Private Jennifer Pitts.

JENNY: Yes, Sergeant?

GRAVES: May I bum a cigarette, Private?

JENNY: I don't have any on me, sir. My apologies.

GRAVES: It's not a crime, Private.

JENNY: Thank you, Sergeant.

GRAVES: I got one a' my own anyways. Would you like one?

JENNY: No thank you, Sergeant. I no longer smoke.

(SGT. GRAVES lights cigarette.)

GRAVES: May I call you Jennifer, Private?

JENNY: *(Slight pause.)* Sergeant?

GRAVES: May I call you Jennifer?

JENNY: *(Slight pause.)* Yes, sir. That's fine.

GRAVES: *(Slight pause.)* Lemme ask you somethin',…Jennifer; what'd they call you back home?

JENNY: I'm sorry, Sergeant?

GRAVES: Your parents. They call you Jennifer?

JENNY: Yes, Sergeant.

GRAVES: I see.

JENNY: Or Jenny.

GRAVES: Or Jenny.

JENNY: Yes, Sergeant.

GRAVES: Your friends?

JENNY: The same, Sergeant.

GRAVES: Your teachers?

JENNY: The same, Sergeant.

GRAVES: Your enemies?

JENNY: *(Slight pause.)* I…I didn't…

GRAVES: Didn't have enemies, right?

JENNY: None that I was aware of, Sergeant.

GRAVES: Well, guess what? Here y'do. You are a soldier in the 451st Military Police Battalion. You let me know that, you let your fellow soldiers know that n'you damn well better let our residents know that, 'cause all it takes is turnin' your back once, okay? Blinkin' at the wrong time. Befriending someone who's schmoozed you into believing that he was innocently abducted at some routine checkpoint, before you end up like the soldier you're replacing; with a medal of honor he never lived to see.

JENNY: Yes, Sergeant.

GRAVES: You are Private Pitts.

JENNY: Yes, Sergeant.

GRAVES: This isn't a resort.

JENNY: Yes, Sergeant.

GRAVES: You're not Jenny the Masseuse, or Jenny comin' in for some Suni motherfucker's 3 o'clock pedicure.

JENNY: Yes, Sergeant.

SGT. GRAVES: You are a soldier, first and foremost.

JENNY: Yes, Sergeant.

GRAVES: Why would you be here if you weren't?

JENNY: Yes, Sergeant.

GRAVES: Hell, why *are* you here, Pitts?

JENNY: To serve and protect…

GRAVES: No, no, not that shit. Why are you here, Private?

JENNY: *(Slight pause.)* Sergeant?

GRAVES: Don't tell me what you think I wana' hear. Tell me what brings a girl from… Where are you from?

JENNY: Halibut, Texas.

GRAVES: You tell me what brings a girl from Halibut, Texas, with no military history in her immediate family, to a country that is a virtual landmine?

JENNY: *(Slight pause.)* Well, I…

GRAVES: No bullshit now.

JENNY: *(Pause.)* Well, sir, I suppose…I'm finding myself.

(A moment, before SGT. GRAVES begins to guffaw…)

GRAVES: Finding yourself.

JENNY: Yes, Sergeant.

GRAVES: Well, shit, Private, most people who claim to be finding themselves don't go to war. They read the fuckin' *I Ching*. They wear robes n'go to Tibet, for Godsakes. Shit, you come to a war-torn nation to find yourself, Private, n'you'll certainly find yourself; with your head blown over the Tigris.

JENNY: *(Slight pause.)* Yes, Sergeant.

GRAVES: *(Slight pause, gently.)* Private, I'm not bustin' your chops 'cause you're a woman,…even a young woman. I've been through this with all the men and women here. This is how I assess your readiness for what's in store.

JENNY: Yes, Sergeant.

GRAVES: Because the fact is that we don't know what's in store. The Department of Defense has given their MO, and we're here to execute it with the utmost efficiency and professionalism. That don't mean we're not learning as we go. Shit, with all my experience as a civilian prison guard, I'm *still* learning as I go. But that's how it should be, because when you learn as you go that means you're honing your instincts in preparation for what you cannot prepare for. *(Slight pause.)* You understand, Private?

JENNY: I do, Sergeant.

GRAVES: Is that so, Private?!

JENNY: It's so, Sergeant!

GRAVES: Is that so, Private Pitts?!!!

JENNY: I'M READY, SERGEANT!!!

GRAVES: *(Slight pause, somewhat impressed.)* Then as far as I'm concerned, you've found yourself already. *(Slight pause, smiles.)* Believe it.

JENNY: Thank you, Sergeant.

> *(A distant explosion as the Lights go out, and into the sound of a static-induced long-distance phone ringing, which stops…)*

OPERATOR: August 23rd, 2003. Collect call from Private Jennifer Pitts.

> *(Lights up on MR. PITTS & MRS. PITTS and JENNY…)*

MRS. PITTS: Are y'sure you're okay, honey?

MR. PITTS: Is there anything else y'need?

JENNY: I'm good.

MRS. PITTS: Y'sure?

JENNY: Yeah, what you've been sendin' is fine.

MRS. PITTS: My God, you sound more like a soldier every time we talk, honey.

MR. PITTS: Well, of course she does, Trish. This ain't the Girl Scouts.

MRS. PITTS: I know, Bill, it's jus'...

MR. PITTS: She's a proud representation of 'er country, is what she is.

MRS. PITTS: Oh, don't I know it.

MR. PITTS: Yep.

MRS. PITTS: Every day they're askin' about ya' here, honey.

MR. PITTS: You're the talk a' the town.

MRS. PITTS: Oh, my God, we didn't even mention the article.

MR. PITTS: That's right.

MRS. PITTS: They wrote an article about ya', honey. In the local paper.

MR. PITTS: They're callin' you a hero, honey.

MR. PITTS: "The Hero of Halibut"

MRS. PITTS: Isn't that somethin'?

JENNY: Yeah, it is.

MR. PITTS: We put it in your latest care package.

MRS. PITTS: You've even helped boost your father's business.

MR. PITTS: Customers who don't even need air conditioners.

MRS. PITTS: Ain't that a hoot'n a holler?

JENNY: Yeah, that's somethin'.

MR. PITTS: *(Slight pause.)* You sure you're okay, honey? We know you're in a different location now...

JENNY: Yeah, I'm fine. Listen, my time's almost up for this call, so...

MR. PITTS: Oh,...alright, darlin'. We know you got a lot goin' on n'all...

MRS, PITTS: We got the cell phones now, so call us whenever you want n'we'll stop on a dime, wherever we are, okay?

JENNY: Okay.

MRS. PITTS: We're so prouda' you, honey.

MR. PITTS: Yes, we are.

MRS. PITTS: We miss you.

MR. PITTS: Yes, we do.

JENNY: Okay, thanks.

MR. PITTS: *(Slight pause.)* Okay, Jenny, I'm gonna' let your mom finish up here, but we'll talk soon.

JENNY: Okay, dad.

MR. PITTS: n'look out for that care package we sent with that article, okay?

JENNY: I will.

MR. PITTS: *(Slight pause.)* You stay well now.

JENNY: *(Slight pause.)* Thanks, dad.

> *(MR. PITTS takes a moment, before going off.)*

MRS. PITTS: Alright, honey. You be safe and God bless, y'hear? I know you've questioned Him…but please know he's with you, whether you think he's there or not.

JENNY: *(Slight pause.)* Okay, I really gotta' go now. The Staff Sergeant needs to see me.

MRS. PITTS: *(Slight pause, a nervous laugh.)* You sound…so different, honey.

JENNY: I gotta' stay strong, mom. This isn't a resort.

MRS. PITTS: *(Slight pause.)* I understand, honey. Your father'n I haven't wanted to get emotional 'cause we figured as much, but…it's just…you're our only child, y'know…?

JENNY: *(Over "y'know…?")* I'm a soldier now, mom. That's the only thing I can be right now. Just try'n understand that, okay?

MRS. PITTS: *(Slight pause.)* Okay. *(Slight pause, barely re-straining.)* We love you.

JENNY: *(Slight pause, restraining…)* I do too. Gotta' go.

(Light out and into a dial tone, which blares and then fades.)

(Lights up on JENNY standing guard with PRIVATE MENDOZA, a young woman of 26. It is approximately 3 months later.)

(A moment. The silence of night lingers.)

MENDOZA: It's fall, right?

JENNY: I don't think they really have seasons here.

MENDOZA: You ain't kiddin'. God, it's fuckin' hot.

JENNY: Want some water?

MENDOZA: Shit, yeah. I'm out. Thanks.

(JENNY hands MENDOZA her canteen.)

(A moment.)

MENDOZA: I'd ask ya' for a cigarette, but I know ya' don't smoke, Pitts.

JENNY: Damn straight.

MENDOZA: Shit, this place would turn a rabbi into a fuckin' heroin addict, n'you don't even smoke. I give ya' credit.

JENNY: Hey, whata' y'gonna' do.

(A moment.)

MENDOZA: Man, what I wouldn't give t'be back home. You don't know.

JENNY: You shittin'?

244

MENDOZA: Are you kiddin' me, Pitts? Look at where we are.

JENNY: Yeah, I know where we are.

MENDOZA: My God, you don't know the value of havin' everything you need within a stone's throw until you're in a place like this. Like real food, not these fuckin' rations. Shit, all the money they're spendin' on this war, n'they give us bad astronaut food.

JENNY: Actually, where I'm from's not too different from here.

MENDOZA: What?

JENNY: Minus the Muslims and the sand.

MENDOZA: Where the hell you from?

JENNY: Halibut, Texas.

MENDOZA: Halibut?

JENNY: Yep.

MENDOZA: Like the fish?

JENNY: Yep. n'not an ocean in sight.

MENDOZA: *(Chuckles.)* Shit, there's irony, right?

JENNY: Hm.

MENDOZA: *(Slight pause.)* Jus' like me bein' here.

JENNY: Whata' y'mean?

MENDOZA: Riskin' my life here jus' so that my kids'n I can have a life back in the states. Ain't that a kick?

JENNY: *(Slight pause.)* I didn't know you had kids.

MENDOZA: Three. *(Slight pause.)* Don't talk about 'em since I been here. Feel like it softens me,...n'they don't want that, right? *(Slight pause.)* I was stupid young. I mean, I don't regret havin' 'em, jus *when* I had 'em'n who I had 'em with.

JENNY: So why are you here 'cause a' that?

MENDOZA: *(Slight pause.)* I was in college, when I was married. Worked full-time too. Then one day I found out my greasy horndog husband was fuckin' around on the side, so I threw his ass out. Had to drop outa' school. Worked 2 fuckin' jobs, then the banks started comin' after me for the student loans I took out. Holy shit, I was so fuckin' depressed. Then a girlfriend told me about joinin' the Army. So I'm like, hey, they'll pay my debt, help me finish college, meantime I'm servin' my country, blah, blah, blah... So aulluvasudden I'm not a single mother in over her head. I'm fuckin' G.I. Jane, y'know? Everyone thinks I'm hot shit.

(A moment.)

JENNY: Okay. So...what happened?

MENDOZA: I miss my kids. I miss home, despite how bad things were. And it sucks here. I mean, shit, patriotism takes y'jus' so far, y'know? Once y'start questionin' that, then everything that's back home starts to hit you right in the face.

JENNY: What's t'question?

MENDOZA: What's t'question?

JENNY: Yeah.

MENDOZA: C'mon, Pitts, a lota' these guys here, it's like they eat red, white'n blue and shit out Bush's head. They don't have families.

JENNY: How d'you know that?

MENDOZA: Well, if they do, they don't seem t'be in any rush t'get back to 'em. Some of 'em, anyway.

JENNY: I don't know about all that. Maybe they're like you. Maybe they gotta' put it outa' mind to stay strong.

(A moment, as they face out.)

MENDOZA: You have any kids, Pitts?

JENNY: *(Slight pause.)* Uh...no.

MENDOZA: I figured you'd be smart enough t'not have 'em too young. You're what, like 21?

JENNY: 20.

MENDOZA: Shit. You gotta' at least be homesick, right? I mean, shit, 20 year old girl, your parents must be...

JENNY: I'm not a girl, Mendoza. They wouldn't let me enlist if I was, y'know?

MENDOZA: Sorry, I wasn't cuttin' ya' down. I mean, God, my mother's probably havin' kanipshins, n'I got 6 years on ya'. I'm jus' sayin'...

JENNY: I know what y'mean. It's fine. *(Slight pause, faces out.)* My parents're concerned n'all, I guess. But actually,...I'm right where I wana' be.

MENDOZA: You gotta' be kiddin'.

JENNY: No, I'm not.

MENDOZA: I mean, I know you're a good soldier'n all but... really?

JENNY: This was a choice, Mendoza. This ain't Vietnam. Everyone chose to come here, regardless a' their circumstances. Right? You did.

MENDOZA: *(Slight pause.)* Yeah, I did. *(A beat, facing out. Tentatively...)* But I didn't choose the shit that's goin' on here.

JENNY: It's war.

MENDOZA: I mean in there.

JENNY: *(Slight pause.)* It's a prison.

MENDOZA: I know.

JENNY: Okay. So, what?

MENDOZA: I mean, you don't think they're startin' to cross a line in there, Pitts?

JENNY: With the prisoners?

MENDOZA: Yeah.

JENNY: *(Slight pause, then firmly.)* No.

MENDOZA: No?

JENNY: They know what they're doin'.

MENDOZA: You think?

JENNY: It's psychological operations, Mendoza. It's from above.

MENDOZA: That's what they say, but...

JENNY: That's what it is. Why should you think otherwise?

MENDOZA: You ever work in a prison?

JENNY: No. Have you?

MENDOZA: No, but...

JENNY: Alright, then...

MENDOZA: But I mean, look, I thought some a' the Shi-ite and Suni jokes were kinda' funny, at first. I admit it. I told some of 'em too. I'm not...y'know, exemptin' myself a' some things here, okay? But don't you think it's startin' t'get a little much? Cursin' at detainees, forcin' 'em t'be without light...?

JENNY: No.

MENDOZA: You don't think...?

JENNY: They're fuckin' terrorists. If they can handle plantin' bombs'n shit, they can handle that.

MENDOZA: They ain't all terrorists.

JENNY: How d'you know they're not?

MENDOZA: They can't be.

JENNY: They can't be? That doesn't make any sense.

MENDOZA: There are a lot a ' detainees here, Pitts. They can't all be the same.

249

JENNY: They at least think the same, n'that's why they're here. Because they've proven themselves t'be a danger to society. You know that.

MENDOZA: Pitts, I don't...

JENNY: *(Over "I don't...)* I mean, shit, how many times a day do we hear *"Allah will punish you."* What d'ya' think that is? It's the same shit those guys said when they took those planes into the Towers'n the Pentagon.

MENDOZA: But even if they all felt that way here, they're prisoners already. Right? Isn't it enough that they're in a cell?

JENNY: Look, Graves worked in a prison back in the states.

MENDOZA: So?

JENNY: So he knows how to deal with prisoners. He'd know if it were too much.

MENDOZA: Pitts, jus' because he worked in a prison don't mean he did it right.

JENNY: *(Slight pause.)* That's a bold insinuation.

MENDOZA: I'm jus' sayin' he may not be the best guy for this place. Shit, not many people would be. I mean, this ain't the same as prison back in the states. I can tell ya' that.

JENNY: I thought you said you didn't work in a prison.

MENDOZA: I didn't, man, but I have a cousin serving 15 years for possession. I mean, he don't say it's a vacation where he's at, but, shit, they got a library, Bible classes, therapy...

JENNY: Whoa, whoa, whoa, Mendoza. First off, you're right. This ain't the same as the states, okay? You think these people are entitled to attend a fuckin' class? Shit, they'll spit at that jus' like one of 'em spit at me today. This is a prison, not a vocational school, okay? n'fuck if they believe in therapy. They swear by their Quran'n that's it.

MENDOZA: Except their Qurans've been confiscated.

JENNY: Damn straight. All it tells 'em apparently is that anyone who doesn't believe what they believe is the fuckin' Devil.

MENDOZA: Yeah, but you…

JENNY: I mean, fuck, Mendoza, this is the Department of Defense's protocol. They got their MO. Period.

MENDOZA: Yeah, but they haven't seen some a' the shit we've seen, Pitts. We've seen some a' these guys ride on the backs of prisoners like mules, for Christ's sake! n'I have a feelin' other crazy shit's gonna' happen soon. n'how're these fuckin' politicians gonna' find out, with them comin' by for their little vanity inspections. Meet'n greet'n that's it. They don't know.

JENNY: Mendoza, look…

MENDOZA: And maybe they do. Maybe they know everything because they don't know what the hell they're doin' either…

JENNY: So tell 'im.

MENDOZA: Whata' y'mean tell 'im?

JENNY: Tell 'im. Question their authority. Tell Graves what you think.

MENDOZA: *(Slight pause.)* What, myself?

JENNY: You're the one who feels this way.

MENDOZA: Yeah, but…

JENNY: What?

MENDOZA: I jus' thought you might think…

JENNY: *(Over "think…")* I don't.

MENDOZA: *(Slight pause.)* It's jus' that…I know you'n Graves're friendly'n all…

JENNY: What the hell's that supposed t'mean?

MENDOZA: Nothin', I'm jus' sayin' you guys get along better than he does with some a' the others…

JENNY: I respect him as my superior.

MENDOZA: Yeah, I know…

JENNY: And he respects me, Mendoza.

MENDOZA: Yeah, I know he does.

JENNY: So what're you gettin' at?

MENDOZA: I'm sayin' that's why I thought it'd be worth bringin' this up with you. I thought, if you felt the same as me, we could get him to…y'know…

JENNY: What?

MENDOZA: I dunno, like…suggest a change in some a' the protocol.

JENNY: The protocol is security and stabilization.

MENDOZA: Yeah, I know, but that shit's just words, Pitts. Everything else is gettin' like an unwritten law here.

JENNY: *We're* the law, Mendoza! And the moment we stop actin' like it is when we lose control a' this place. Now why don't you nip this in the bud before someone hears ya'. Alright?

MENDOZA: Yeah, that's what I gotta' worry about now, right? I gotta' hope that the others don't hear me questioning…

JENNY: Look, Mendoza, you're endangering yourself and the rest of us by thinkin' this way. So stop doin' it, alright? Just keep your head on straight, n'if it helps, try not thinkin' about your kids.

(JENNY faces back out, as MENDOZA looks at her.)

MENDOZA: They got you conditioned pretty well, don't they.

JENNY: Look, Mendoza, this ain't the Girl Scouts…

MENDOZA: I know what this is…

JENNY: *(Over "what this is…")* Drop it, alright?!

MENDOZA: Look at you. Younger than me n'you're tellin' me to drop it. You got some…

JENNY: Age doesn't mean two shits here, Mendoza. I know why I'm here, n'you're forgettin'.

MENDOZA: *(Pause.)* You know, maybe it takes a mother t'have some sympathy. I guess that's to my disadvantage as far as my survival here. Maybe if you had a kid, you'd be able to see things through different eyes but, as it turns out, you may as well have a fuckin' dick.

JENNY: You can kiss my ass, you insubordinate piece a' shit…!

MENDOZA: *(Over "pieca' shit...!)* Insubordinate...?! You ain't my superior...!

JENNY: *(Over "superior...")* You're not doin' anyone any favors bein' here, least of all your fuckin' country!!!

MENDOZA: Look, Pitts, you may think your Miss Patriotic Bitch, but you may understand less why you're here than I do, okay...?

JENNY: *(Over "than I do, okay...?")* I know why I'm here.

MENDOZA: Why?

JENNY: I know why the fuck I'm here...!

MENDOZA: *(Over "...the fuck...")* Why?!

JENNY: *(Unhinged!)* I'M REPRESENTING MY FUCKING COUNTRY!!! I'm here 'cause I represent a country that was attacked by fuckers who feel the same way as these fuckers in here. I'm here 'cause I'm tryin' to make people who live in fear sleep a little easier 'cause if it ain't for us, it's Marshall Law, okay?! Every cretin does what they want n'innocent people die. These assholes are safer than if they were free in their own damn country. Are you fuckin' kiddin' me?!!! They don't know how good they got it, with crazy shits blowin' themselves up as often as you can blink!!!

MENDOZA: Pitts, I'm jus' tryin' to...

JENNY: *(Over "tryin' to...")* What?! What the fuck are you sayin' now?!!!

MENDOZA: *(Slight pause.)* I jus' thought...bein' a woman, we'd be able t'see some things the same...

JENNY: *(Over "some things...")* Fuck bein' a woman! The U.S. is a progressive country, Mendoza. We're not women doin' a man's job anymore: We're soldiers, d'you understand?! You wana' look at it like you're a little girl outa' your element, then that's the quickest way to get your throat cut by these sand-swallowin' motherfuckers who couldn't care less about you, your country or your fucking kids!!! Now you make a decision and you make it right fuckin' now; either request a transfer or SHAPE THE FUCK UP!!!

> *(JENNY maintains her intense gaze at MENDOZA, who is almost immobilized. JENNY slowly turns out.)*
>
> *(After a moment, MENDOZA too faces out.)*
>
> *(The lights fade out and into the sounds of distant gunfire, explosions..., as an exclusive light appears on DEFENSE SECRETARY, as if at a televised news conference...)*

DEFENSE SECRETARY: *(With grand assurance.)* Despite rumors to the contrary, the American people should take comfort in knowing that the US Military is handling the growing number of prisoner acquisitions with greater civility than if they were imprisoned by their own military. That you can rest assured.

> *(The final word echoes, as all sounds fade...)*
>
> *(Lights up on GRAVES and JENNY, in Graves' office.)*

GRAVES: Thanks for comin' in.

JENNY: Of course, Sergeant.

GRAVES: I know things can get a little overwhelming around here so I jus' wanted to check in with ya'.

JENNY: Thank you, Sergeant.

GRAVES: *(Slight pause.)* You're okay?

JENNY: *(Slight pause.)* Yes, Sergeant.

GRAVES: This is…an unusual environment for the average person. Even the average soldier, y'know? We're claustrophobic as all get out. We're, in a sense, closed off from civilization, really, 'cause God knows what's in here ain't, right?

JENNY: Yes, Sergeant.

GRAVES: *(Slight pause.)* I jus' wana' make sure that…you're still on board with what our intent is here.

JENNY: *(Slight pause.)* I… I'm sorry, sir, but…have I given you reason to feel otherwise…?

GRAVES: No, Private. But…there's some rumblin' goin' on. I won't go the extent of saying that there's dissention in the ranks here, but…I'm jus' sensing some weakness with certain people. *(Slight pause.)* Have you heard things?

JENNY: *(A beat.)* Dissention?

GRAVES: Or…a close proximity thereof?

JENNY: *(Slight pause.)* No, Sergeant.

GRAVES: *(Slight pause.)* You're sure.

JENNY: Yes, Sergeant.

GRAVES: *(Slight pause.)* What was goin' on with Mendoza last night?

JENNY: Sergeant?

GRAVES: Chambers said he heard you guys screamin' at each other while standing guard.

JENNY: Um, I…I…

GRAVES: You know what I'm speaking about, yes?

JENNY: Uh, yes, Sergeant, but…it had nothing to do with what you're speaking of.

GRAVES: It didn't.

JENNY: It was jus' an animated discussion.

GRAVES: Unrelated.

JENNY: Yes, Sergeant.

GRAVES: Really.

JENNY: Yes, Sergeant.

GRAVES: *(Slight pause.)* I don't think that's the case, Private.

JENNY: *(Slight pause.)* I… Sergeant?

GRAVES: I don't feel that's the case.

JENNY: I… I mean… Has Mendoza told you something different, 'cause…?

GRAVES: Actually, I haven't spoken to Mendoza. Because I don't need to. I know what was said.

JENNY: *(Slight pause.)* Sergeant,…

GRAVES: Private, let me say something to you, alright? You've exhibited yourself thus far to be an efficient, tough-minded, resourceful soldier, with clear intention as to our mission here. But you cannot defend someone whose ideals are not equal to yours because that is a sign of weakness that you have thus far evaded. We all gotta' be on the same page here, y'understand?

JENNY: Yes, Sergeant.

GRAVES: There cannot be unity when there is disparity. And the moment that there becomes an exposed chink in our armor is when these prisoners can exploit us. You don't think these people are lookin' for any window to flee this place? You don't think they're waitin' for you to make one wrong move and take your life?

JENNY: I understand, Sergeant.

GRAVES: I don't ever wana' hear you coverin' the ass of someone who can put all our lives in jeopardy!

JENNY: Sergeant,…

GRAVES: *Your* life!

JENNY: Yes, Sergeant…

GRAVES: You didn't come all the way from… Where the hell you from again?!

JENNY: Halibut, Texas…

GRAVES: You didn't come all the way from Halibut, Texas to get killed as a result of a treasonous fellow MP from wherever the hell *she's* from! You understand?!

JENNY: I…I understand, Sergeant.

GRAVES: *(Slight pause, calmly.)* You understand why we do what we do, right?

JENNY: *(Slight pause.)* With…the prisoners?

GRAVES: You understand.

JENNY: It's Psychological Operations, Sergeant. Direct orders.

GRAVES: *(Slight pause.)* That's correct. *(Slight pause.)* These are evil people, Private. I know you're cognizant a' that fact. But it's also important t'know that, even if we weren't authorized by the Department of Defense, we'd damn well still be entitled to show them our displeasure from time to time. There's no shame in a little humiliation because they've earned it. And we've earned the right to invoke it. I know you understand that.

JENNY: *(Slight pause.)* Yes, Sergeant.

GRAVES: They're in better care with us than on their own streets, with how things are now. Believe me.

JENNY: I understand, Sergeant.

GRAVES: *(Slight pause, a half-smile.)* You have fun with it, right?

JENNY: Well, I mean, Sergeant, maybe…maybe "fun" is not…the most accurate term I'd…

GRAVES: C'mon, Pitts. You don't have to suppress anything with me. These people took an arm'n a leg from my brother in the last war. Don't think they'd mind takin' the same from you. Your folks too, if they had the chance.

(A moment, JENNY weakly nods.)

(Gently…) Look, you can feel any way you wana' feel about it. I respect you too much t'not allow you that. I'm jus' sayin' don't feel that you have to deprive yourself if you feel like crackin' a grin.

JENNY: *(Slight pause.)* Al…alright, Sergeant.

GRAVES: It's cathartic. Priests pray and the Hari Krishnas meditate. We serve and protect, n'have to be unwavering in doin' so. But a smile at a job well done is ok too.

JENNY: *(Slight pause.)* Alright, Sergeant.

GRAVES: Good. *(A beat, a pleased grin.)* We're gonna' take some pictures soon.

JENNY: Pictures, Sergeant?

GRAVES: Yep. Got a coupla' cameras. Chambers is an amateur photog, so he's up for it. Delucci too. Strip 'em down n'stack 'em up!

JENNY: Stack 'em up?

GRAVES: Mhm.

JENNY: Stack…what up, exactly, Sergeant?

GRAVES: You've always been a demon for details, Pitts. *(Smiles.)* The prisoners!

JENNY: *(Slight pause.)* The…the prisoners?

GRAVES: Oh, yeah.

JENNY: *(Slight pause.)* Uh, that's… Wow…um…

GRAVES: Yes, Private?

JENNY: *(Slight pause.)* Who…who are the prisoners you had in mind?

GRAVES: A few of the insurgents. A couple who shot some MPs. One of 'em even spit at you from his cell. Remember that lovely gentleman?

JENNY: You...you weren't even there when it happened.

GRAVES: You think a prisoner expectoratin' on my favorite MP is gonna' slip past me?

(A moment, as JENNY weakly grins...)

GRAVES: Hey, we're entitled. Don't y'think?

JENNY: *(Slight pause.)* Yes, sir.

GRAVES: *You're* entitled.

JENNY: *(Slight pause, almost flattered.)* Thank you, Sergeant.

(A moment, before GRAVES takes a step toward JENNY...)

GRAVES: You're entitled to other things too, y'know?

JENNY: *(Slight pause, a weak smile.)* Sergeant?

GRAVES: *(Slight pause.)* You're pretty special.

JENNY: *(Slight pause.)* I...thank you.

GRAVES: It's true. Hey, you know I'm not much of a bullshitter.

JENNY: *(Slowly drawn in...)* I respect that, Sergeant.

GRAVES: 'Scuse my French.

JENNY: That's okay.

GRAVES: *(Slight pause.)* You have a boyfriend back in the states?

JENNY: *(Slight pause.)* No, Sergeant.

GRAVES: *(A grin.)* Hm. Well, I think even if you had one, he wouldn't be enough for you, Private.

JENNY: *(Slight pause, unclear.)* Wha…whata' you mean, Sergeant?

GRAVES: *(Tenderly.)* I jus' think, if you'll permit me to say, that…you're a special young lady. I don't know too much about you but…from what you've told me and from what I've gathered, I get that you've been unfulfilled. Emotionally, I mean. C'mon, it takes a helluva woman to come to a place like this when she doesn't have to, y'know? Hell, I know everyone's got their reasons, but…in your case,…I think it stems from tryin' to fill somethin'. Somethin' that'll make you feel whole. Give yourself somethin' that…another young man your age doesn't have the capacity to give you. Because you're special. Truly. *(Slight pause.)* I know…I know you've wanted a father's love…on your terms. You've wanted him to love you for who you've created yourself to be and not what he wanted you to be. And that'll always make your desire for love…strong. An older man can…give ya' that, y'know?

(A moment, as they look at each other.)

I've seen the way you look at me,…Jenny. Would it be…a misinterpretation on my part if I assumed that…you kinda' like me? Would that…be fair?

(A considerable moment.)

JENNY: *(Almost breathless…)* It would.

(A moment, before GRAVES takes a small step

262

towards JENNY...)

(After a moment, she does the same.)

(Eventually they move towards each other slowly... and gently kiss...as their light fades...)

(In a dim light, we see a silhouette of a group of prisoners, and 2 MPS on either side, CHAMBERS and DELUCCI.)

CHAMBERS: Alright, you Arab fucks!

DELUCCI: Today is your special day!

CHAMBERS: You do what you're ordered to do and we won't have t'kick the livin' Shi-ite out of ya', alright?!

DELUCCI: The Suni you do what we tell ya', the Suni we can get started.

CHAMBERS: You're gonna' be models, man!

DELUCCI: How about that?

CHAMBERS: Fuckin' Suni-super models.

(They both laugh...)

DELUCCI: Right. You're gonna be famous. Ain't that somethin'?

CHAMBERS: Ain't that somethin', douchebags?!

DELUCCI: YOU HEAR US, MOTHERFUCKERS?!

CHAMBERS: YOU STAND AT ATTENTION, YOU PIECES A' FUCKIN' SHIT, BEFORE WE STICK A ROD UP YOUR FUCKIN' ASSES!!!!

(The silhouetted prisoners stand at attention, as Chambers and Delucci observe with satisfaction...)

CHAMBERS: That's right.

(Light change, as CHAMBERS enters with camera. GRAVES confidently stands beside a visually trepidatious JENNY.)

CHAMBERS: Okay, got some of our models together. You guys ready to go-go-go?

(GRAVES looks at JENNY, senses her uneasiness, before gesturing to CHAMBERS to step away, which he does.)

GRAVES: *(A beat.)* You ready?

JENNY: *(Slight pause.)* I'm really not sure. I don't...

GRAVES: C'mon, no one's gettin' hurt. I told ya', it'll be fun.

JENNY: I jus'... This isn't why I came...

GRAVES: I know.

JENNY: I'm just...

GRAVES: I know. You came t'find yourself, right? And you did. You're a soldier. You're an American. n'you're a woman with bigger balls than most men I know, okay?

JENNY: I'm just really not sure about all this...

GRAVES: Hey, look at me a second.

JENNY: *(Over "look at me a second...")* I'm sorry, I jus'…

GRAVES: Don't worry about it, it's all good. Jus' look me in the eyes, okay?

(She does, as he gently takes her by the shoulders…)

Look, I would never put you in harm's way. I have way too much respect for you. You know that, right?

(She tepidly nods.)

And it's because a' that respect that I asked you to be a part a' this, okay? You represent the best of us here, Jenny. This isn't a privilege I'd offer to just anyone. Remember what I told you; you're special. And you are entitled to this. We risk our lives every damn day, okay? This is just…a little release. That's all.

(She weakly nods.)

You don't have to do anything you don't want to do. *(Slight pause.)* It's just…I thought this'd be a fun thing to do together. *(Slight pause.)* I really… I have feelings for ya'. Okay? *(A beat.)* And you…have 'em for me, right?

(She slowly forms a smile...)

JENNY: You know I do.

GRAVES: *(Smiles.)* Okay, then?

(JENNY takes a moment, then nods with a certain conviction. GRAVES suddenly turns, …)

GRAVES: BRING 'EM IN!

CHAMBERS: ALRIGHT, LET'S DO THIS!!!

(We faintly hear JENNY's recorded voice reciting the self-composed military mantra – below, which is soon overlapped by the NEWSCASTER, in an exclusive light.)

(Under the following, a dimly lit stage reveals GRAVES, JENNY, CHAMBERS - with camera - and DELUCCI crudely orchestrating several prisoners into a variety of crude poses, each one concluded by a camera flash. With each quick flash comes a different pose; JENNY standing over the prisoner pile with a gun, ...then with a broad smile, then a thumbs up, then with a prisoner on a leash, then with GRAVES.)

(Each pose with GRAVES becomes subtly more intimate, to where eventually it is as if they are unaware that they are behind a stack of prisoners...)

JENNY's VOICE: *(In a continuous loop, which fades out by the 3rd time.)* "I'm here to serve and protect my country to the very best of my ability while upholding the standards of moral integrity, courage and valor that are the vital components of the United States army." *(Repeats continually under Newscaster...)*

NEWSCASTER: *(Overlapping by the first repetition of above...)* Over the last few months, there have been ongoing rumors with regards to prisoner treatment in Iraq, just outside of Baghdad. These speculations can now more accurately be referred to as fact, which has ignited a federal investigation into what seems, at the very least, to encompass overzealous treatment of prisoners by U.S. Military Police personnel. Prompted by various photos which have come to light depicting several MPs posing with prisoners in a bevy of degrading poses, the U. S Army and the Defense Secretary claim that they did not in any way endorse or have knowledge of such actions and seek to pinpoint those responsible. There are several who have heretofore been identified in the photos, including Staff Sergeant Reginald Graves and, most prominently, Private Jennifer Pitts of Halibut, Texas, who, in one photo, can be seen giving a thumbs up before a stacked pile of naked Iraqi prisoners, in addition to several disarmingly intimate poses with Graves.

(The Newscast and Jenny's mantra abruptly cease, as GRAVES poses on one knee before a standing JENNY in front of the prisoner pile...)

GRAVES: Would you marry me, Jenny?

JENNY: I... Oh, my... Yes. Yes!

(They embrace and kiss – a FLASH! - before the stage goes black, except on NEWSCASTER, who continues...)

NEWSCASTER: It is unclear how the photos were leaked, though the Defense Secretary vows to take immediate action, saying quote;

(Immediate Light on DEFENSE SECRETARY...)

DEFENSE SECRETARY: *(With heightened indignance.)* These photos shed light on a situation that we knew nothing about. But knowing what we now know, I vow to bring the soldiers responsible to justice for their reckless disregard for military protocol and the heinous contempt for human life that directly opposes what is the very mantra of the United States Military!

(An explosion!)

(An exclusive light comes up on JENNY, as in the opening scene. A moment.)

MILITARY JUDGE: Private, before we conclude the proceedings here today, I wanted to take this time to allow you the opportunity of speaking on your own behalf. If there is anything you feel you'd like to leave this court with, without provocation of questions or cross-examination, you may speak now.

(A moment, JENNY contains a wealth of emotion.)

Have you anything you wish to say?

*(A moment, before JENNY struggles to simply open
    her mouth...)*

Private? Have you anything you'd like to say?

(A moment, as she attempts to speak...but cannot...)

Private?

(A moment.)

JENNY: An old friend a' mine once said, *"Too bad there ain't
no war."* Because...he was raised to believe that...in times of
war, we are best defined. Otherwise, we're jus'...strugglin'
through life, tryin' to find who we really are. Hoping we'll be
accepted...and loved for...who we discover ourselves to be.
(Slight pause.) I was...I was inspired when our country was attacked, your Honor. I...I found somethin' in myself that no one
coulda' seen, and I was...I was proud a' that. I guess...you can
say I kinda' felt like...Joan of Arc. Not jus'...not just a rebel this
time,...but someone who...who really stood for somethin'.
(Slight pause, with further anguish.) I...I participated...in...in
awful things...and...and for that...I'm very sorry. At first, I...I
believed that these were orders from above, authorized tactics to
lower prisoner resistance and obtain information...but, ulti-
mately,...it became...it...it became... *(Slight pause, barely
restrains her emotions.)* Somethin' else. *(Slight pause.)* A few
men'n women who...got themselves to believin' that they were
laws unto themselves. *(Slight pause, emotionally but com-
mitedly.)* And I...am among them.

*(JENNY's light goes out in sync with the sounds of a
    most violent car crash!!!)*

THE DISHONORABLE DISCHARGE OF PRIVATE PITTS

(Lights up on several dimly lit Halibut TOWNSPEOPLE, including Mr. & Mrs. Pitts…)

TOWNIE #1: On the morning of a day in Texas,

TOWNIE #2: as her parents drove to work in their car,

TOWNIE #3: the news came over the radio;

TOWNIE #4: sentenced and dishonorably discharged.

MRS. PITTS: Taken aback by the news,

MR. PITTS: her father swerved into the opposing lane.

TOWNIE #5: He'd drive head on into the oncoming truck;…

ALL: All would die that day.

(The Lights fade on the TOWNIES and come up on JENNY behind bars, at a Military Prison in the States. She sits, holding her stomach in a near fetal position. MAN & WOMAN have stepped forward from being TOWNIES and now appear before her cell, respectively as GUARDS # 2 and #1.)

(A moment.)

GUARD #1: One year and a Dishonorable Discharge.

GUARD #2: Well, fuck, it's not like she's alone. They got like 9 others scattered around.

GUARD #1: Why does it seem like she'll be serving more time than any of them?

GUARD #2: Hey, she wanted t'be the fuckin' covergirl.

GUARD #1: I don't know that she *wanted* it, Joe. Christ…!

GUARD #2: Come on. 1 year? It's a slap.

GUARD #1: Yeah, and after a year they throw her to the wolves.

GUARD #2: Fuckin' A. Let 'em rip her to shreds. She deserves it.

GUARD # 1: Joe, c'mon…

GUARD #2: No, don't gimme that shit! It's because of her everyone in the world thinks the US Army is the equivalent of the fuckin' mafia, for Godsakes.

GUARD #1: I'm not sayin' she's innocent. I jus' think she was a patsy.

GUARD #2: Because she's a woman.

GUARD #1: No, because it's…

GUARD #2: *("because it's…")* Fuckin' shit, she's in the photos pointing at these guys dicks. Naked prisoners. What the hell was goin' on there?

GUARD #1: You don't have to tell me. I just think she was coerced. 20 years old, barely over 5 feet… Come on…

GUARD #2: *(Over "Come on…")* I don't care if she was a fuckin' elf, okay? What're you doin' in these photos, for Godsakes?

GUARD #1: I'm just saying Graves is a shit.

GUARD #2: So? How d'you know he's a bigger shit than she is?

GUARD #1: He had sex with 3 soldiers while he was stationed in Kuwait. He had a record before he even enlisted...

GUARD #2: So what's the difference? He's serving time.

GUARD #1: He shouldn'ta even had his post, Joe. God, he was Staff Sergeant. He was in charge a' that wing...

GUARD #2: (Over "...a' that wing...") Hey, if it helps you, I have nothing but contempt for all those fuckers. Okay? Man, woman or prisoner. They're all shit t'me. But because Pitts is here, she can take a little a' my heat.

GUARD #1: What're you talkin' about?

GUARD #2: You heard me.

GUARD #1: Jesus, her parents just got killed...

GUARD #2: So?

GUARD #1: So how about a little fucking compassion?

GUARD #2: She hasn't earned my compassion, okay? Who the fuck is she?! My father's got cirrhosis of the fuckin' liver. Y'think she gives two shits about that? Now I'm not gonna'...

JENNY: (Over "Now I'm not gonna'...", while holding stomach.) I'm...I'm sorry.

GUARD #2: What?!

JENNY: (Slight pause.) Did...did you say my parents...got killed?

GUARD #1: (Slight pause.) You didn't know, Pitts?

JENNY: I...they're dead...?

GUARD #2: They're dead, Pitts. Okay? They're dead.

GUARD #1: Joe, stop it...!

GUARD #2: And I'm sure they were real prouda' you!

GUARD #1: Joe, that's enough! Back the fuck off...!

GUARD #2: She's a pieca' shit!

GUARD #1: *(Over "...pieca' shit...")* Back off, Joe!

JENNY: *(As if the pain has grown...)* I...I need to see the physician, I think...

GUARD #2 & #1: Yeah, nice try. / Are you okay, Pitts?

JENNY: My...my stomach, I'm...I need to see...

GUARD #2: Please, she's fine.

GUARD #1: Joe, she could really be hurting...!

　　　(JENNY drops to the floor....)

　　　(Lights Out and Up on JENNY who sits atop table. PHYSICIAN stands before her with clipboard, barely looking at JENNY throughout...)

PHYSICIAN: And you have no idea what this stems from?

JENNY: *(Slight pause.)* Well, I thought...maybe stress.

PHYSICIAN: Stress.

JENNY: I mean, I've been...goin' through quite a bit lately, so...

PHYSICIAN: You've been pregnant before.

JENNY: *(Slight pause.)* I...what? No, I...

PHYSICIAN: Yes, you have.

JENNY: But...no, that's...

PHYSICIAN: I used to be an OBGYN, okay? I can tell these things.

JENNY: *(Pause.)* I...okay. Yes, I...

PHYSICIAN: So I figured you'd be familiar with this feeling, yes?

JENNY: *(Slight pause.)* Are you saying I'm...I'm...?

PHYSICIAN: Yes. Just over 2 months now.

JENNY: Two...two...

PHYSICIAN: Yes.

(A moment, as JENNY absorbs this...)

PHYSICIAN: *(Jots on clipboard...)* You know the father, I assume?

JENNY: *(Slight pause, adrift...)* Yes,...I know 'im.

PHYSICIAN: Well, you should tell him. Is he still serving?

JENNY: *(Slight pause.)* In prison. Fort Leavenworth, I heard.

PHYSICIAN: Oh, lovely. A marriage made in purgatory.

JENNY: We're not married. We're not gettin' married.

PHYSICIAN: *(Jots…)* Oh, even better.

JENNY: We were engaged. Before…
(She gazes off, despondently.)

PHYSICIAN: Yes, well, still'n all, you're pregnant. There's your diagnosis. *(…she starts to leave…)*

JENNY: I…what…what can I do?

PHYSICIAN: What can you do?

JENNY: I…I mean, I'm…I have to serve my sentence. I can't…how can I have a baby here? How can I…I can't be…

PHYSICIAN: Pitts, I think you're confusing me with a social worker, okay? If you're having a crisis of conscience over your inability to raise a child, then I suggest you speak with the chaplain. All I can offer you here is aspirin. Now is there anything else?

(JENNY is speechless.)

Pitts?

JENNY: Ye…yes.

PHYSICIAN: Anything else?

(JENNY is unable to speak.)

(The Lights change, as JENNY, unable to make eye contact initially, sits awkwardly before CHAPLAIN, who also sits.)

(A considerable moment.)

CHAPLAIN: Jenny? *(Slight pause.)* Would you like to say something?

JENNY: *(Slight pause.)* It's been...so long. I don't...I don't know where to start.

CHAPLAIN: Well, don't worry about formalities. This isn't confession. Just say what's on your mind. Okay?

(A moment.)

Jenny?

JENNY: *(Slight pause, a weak smile.)* It's funny.

CHAPLAIN: What is?

JENNY: That I've been...dishonorably discharged.

CHAPLAIN: Why is that?

JENNY: I don't mean...laughin' funny. I mean...

CHAPLAIN: I understand. Why is it funny?

JENNY: (*Pause, with a degree of shame.*) I was born dead.

CHAPLAIN: I'm sorry?

JENNY: I was stillborn.

CHAPLAIN: Well,...there's certainly nothing dishonorable in that.

JENNY: *(Slight pause, with barely contained emotion.)* I think...I think there is.

CHAPLAIN: (*Slight pause.*) Why would you think such a thing?

(*A moment.*)

JENNY: When I…when I was little,…everybody's eyes seemed so kind. But it was…it was weird, y'know? It wasn't… It never felt like it was at me. (*Slight pause.*) It was like they were lookin' at something divine or… It didn't matter what I was or who I was. I survived death. I was a "miracle". That's what they saw. (*Pause.*) Father,…I never told anyone this. I…I saw somethin' when I was born.

CHAPLAIN: (*Slight pause.*) And…what was that, Jenny?

JENNY: A light. I saw…just a nice, comforting light beaming right at me.

(*A moment.*)

CHAPLAIN: Why have you never told anyone that?

JENNY: (*Slight pause.*) I dunno'. I guess it seemed like the moment I drew breath, my parents were all over me. I mean, they doted on me so much that I…I guess I didn't have time to take in what it really was that I saw. They jus' wanted me to love God for givin' me life,…so that's what I did. But…eventually, I figured it out.

CHAPLAIN: And what was that?

JENNY: (*Slight pause, deeply.*) That it was…it was God rejecting me. And what can be more dishonorable than that?

CHAPLAIN: Jenny,…surviving death is not a rejection by God.

JENNY: (*Sharply, with great emotion.*) Then what the hell is it, Father?!

CHAPLAIN: (*Slight pause.*) It's confirmation that your life has value here on earth.

JENNY: I don't believe that.

CHAPLAIN: Jenny, you have to...

JENNY: That doesn't make any sense!

CHAPLAIN: Why doesn't that make sense to you?

JENNY: *(With building emotion...)* Because I'm here! I'm in prison. I contributed nothin' to this earth except to cause distress. I...I participated in awful things in Baghdad. I didn't say anything. I didn't speak up. I allowed prisoners to be...to be humiliated. I think...I think I'm responsible for my parents' death, my friend Chad's death, my friend Sherry's... And...and...and, oh shit...

CHAPLAIN: Jenny,...

JENNY: Oh, shit, Father...

CHAPLAIN: Jenny,...

JENNY: I GAVE MY BABY AWAY!!! Oh, shit...my...my baby....! Will...William...

    (JENNY breaks down, convulsively sobbing...)

    (CHAPLAIN extends his hand, but JENNY resists.)

CHAPLAIN: Jenny. (*Slight pause.*) Jenny, it's okay.

    (Eventually, JENNY gathers.)

    (A moment.)

CHAPLAIN: So you've had a child?

JENNY: *(Slight pause.)* When I was 16. I had t'... I had t'put him up for adoption.

CHAPLAIN: *(Slight pause.)* Perhaps that was best.

JENNY: *(Slight pause, facing him.)* And now?

CHAPLAIN: *(Slight pause.)* You're pregnant now?

JENNY: *(Slight pause.)* 2 months.

CHAPLAIN: *(Slight pause.)* This happened...?

JENNY: My superior.

CHAPLAIN: *(Slight pause.)* I see.

JENNY: *(Slight pause.)* After I was born, the doctors told my parents that...later on I may experience adverse affects from...bein' dead. Because of the lack of oxygen I had for a time. They said maybe retardation, autism... Nothin' took. *(Slight pause.)* They never mentioned bad judgment.

CHAPLAIN: You're human, Jenny.

JENNY: I'm a little worse than that, Father.

CHAPLAIN: Jenny,...no one of this earth is without sin. No one is without fault. And sometimes the faults happen to be on a larger stage, but...

JENNY: You don't understand, Father. I don't want sympathy. I don't wana' be released. Okay? I either wana' serve a life sentence or die. There's nothin' else for me out there.

CHAPLAIN: That's not true.

JENNY: Yes, it is, Father.

CHAPLAIN: Jenny, the greatest virtue within everyone is the ability of overcoming our pain. The pain we've inflicted and the pain we've absorbed.

JENNY: I don't think I can anymore.

CHAPLAIN: I think you can...

JENNY: Father, please...I can't have this baby!

CHAPLAIN: *(Slight pause.)* Why can't you?

JENNY: *(Slight pause, choked up...)* Because I'm here.

CHAPLAIN: You're not here forever. And while you're here, arrangements can be made so that your child...

JENNY: It's not just that. When I'm released. I don't...I don't have anybody. I don't have a family. I don't have friends. It'll be like I'm born into the world again, only this time I'll have a child that I can't support.

CHAPLAIN: How do you know that you can't?

JENNY: I... Everyone knows my face'n... Who'll hire me t'do anything? n'I don't wana' put my child through...

CHAPLAIN: Jenny,...right now you're not in the frame of mind to think that far ahead. Give yourself time. You have time, y'know. Consider it a gift. *(Slight pause.)* And let God work through you.

JENNY: *(A beat.)* God won't touch me.

CHAPLAIN: That's not true.

JENNY: It's true.

CHAPLAIN: Jenny,…don't be afraid to believe in Him. *(Slight pause.)* Regardless,…He believes in you.

(JENNY turns to him slowly, tearfully…)

JENNY: Why…why would you think such a thing?

CHAPLAIN: *(Slight pause, with a half-smile.)* I just do. Of course, I respect that you may have to discover this on your own, as you've discovered other things in your life. Though…I will say that if someone you don't believe in believes in you,…then at the very least you should believe in yourself. Don't you think? *(Slight pause.)* Have you ever read the Quran, Jenny?

JENNY: *(Pause, with great shame.)* We burned a few.

CHAPLAIN: *(Pause, digesting this.)* Well, there's one line that goes: *"God is within those who persevere."*

(He approaches JENNY… Slight pause.)

You made mistakes…and you're sorry for them, yes?

JENNY: *(Tearfully…)* Yes…

CHAPLAIN: And you're alive to make up for them. You'll serve your sentence, you'll be released…and you'll figure it out from there. *(Slight pause.)* You were born unto this earth for a reason, Jenny. You've been searching for why,…and you're not alone in your search. And, let me tell you, the ones who search…and the ones who persevere…are the ones who are alive. Truly…alive. *(Slight pause.)* Maybe that's something you can pass on.

(JENNY remains still, looking at the CHAPLAIN, who smiles…as the lights fade.)

THE DISHONORABLE DISCHARGE OF PRIVATE PITTS

(An exclusive light appears on SHERRY, 23, as we see JENNY in her cell reading letter.)

SHERRY: Dear Jenny,

It's Sherry, girl! I know this must be weird to be getting this from me, especially considering where you are now. But I'm at least glad I found you. I've heard you won't be imprisoned long, but I so hope you're doing okay. I had tried your parents' number a few weeks back, but it says it's disconnected. Maybe I wrote it down wrong but...I did try. Did they move? I would've tried earlier but...I think I needed to keep my past in that maternity home and felt, if I contacted you,...it may be too much for me.

I know you understand what I'm talking about.

I was in a real bad way after you last saw me. My parents didn't want anything to do with me. I got in bad relationships, did drugs, got pregnant again, got an abortion... Yeah, the whole shitty en-chilada. I was just...really lost.

But then one day, I came across this little piece of paper you gave me. I'll bet you don't even remember.

You said you'd come up with it when you were little. You wrote it down and gave it to me before I left. I even remember you saying, *"I don't even believe this shit anymore, but maybe it'll do something for ya'."*

I didn't read it then. Never wanted to because, again, I thought, whatever it was, it'd be way too painful for me.

Anyway, just as I was about to take a handful of pills from my purse,...here's what magically fell out:

> *I love God and He loves me.*
> *He brought me into this world*
> *to spread love and peace.*

Among all His children,
one thing should be known;
when you give yourself to God,
you're never alone.

I guess timing was everything, huh? There it was, on a wrinkly old post-it note.

Hey, I'm not saying I'm a gung-ho Christian now or anything. Believe me, I'm not. Actually, I don't even know if I fully believe in God. It was more knowing that there was someone who gave enough of a shit about me to hand me that piece of paper.

Anyway,...it helped.

Shortly after reading that, I just started to get some focus in my life. I left my last prick boyfriend and got my own place. You're welcome to visit or stay with me anytime. I'm not in Texas anymore though. I'm in New freakin' Jersey. Ain't that a hoot? By the shore. It's nice. I like it. The sea air is soooo invigorating.

I'm teaching art to pre-schoolers. How funny, huh? I love it. They're good kids. One day I'll have one of my own,...or at least try to contact the one I gave up. Just to be in touch. She was such a beautiful girl.

Anyway, look me up when you get out. I'd love to see you. If it's too much, I'll understand. In any case, I at least wanted to tell you...thanks for saving my life, Jenny.

Regardless of what they're saying about you,...you're my hero.

Love,
Sherry

> *(SHERRY's light goes out, as we hear a cell door opening...)*

THE DISHONORABLE DISCHARGE OF PRIVATE PITTS

*(We soon see JENNY being escorted by GUARD #2 &
#3 as GUARD #1 hands JENNY her baby.)*

*(A moment, as JENNY looks at her, a tepid smile, be-
fore…)*

JENNY: Is…is there anything else I need to do?

GUARD #2: Your year's up. You're free to go.

*(A moment, before JENNY takes a few steps, as the Lights
change to the outside world. She is still for a moment,
with baby in her arms. For the moment, she looks out
nervously, almost appearing hopeful, before the cell door
slams shut! Immediately, dimly lit INTERVIEWERS
speak out, who Jenny failingly attempts to answer…)*

INTERVIEWER 1: I'm sorry, what did you say your name
was?

INTERVIEWER 2: Jennifer Pitts?!

INTERVIEWER 3: We're not looking right now and, frankly,
even if we were, we certainly wouldn't be looking for *you*.

INTERVIEWER 1: For Godsakes, please leave.

INTERVIEWER 2: How dare you even ask!

INTERVIEWER 3: Shouldn't you be in prison?!

INTERVIEWER 1: How do you think it would look having you
on the floor?!

INTERVIEWER 2: All day customers'll be saying *"Is that who
I think it is? Is that who I think it is?"*

INTERVIEWERS 1, 2 & 3: *"Is that who I think it is?! Is that who I think it is?!"*

TAUNTER # 1: Holy shit, is that her?!

> *(Light change and we see JENNY amidst an array of dimly lit TAUNTERS from various regions of the U.S.)*

> *(*The following builds in tempo and intensity, as JENNY's attempts to evade…)*

TAUNTER #2: Yeah, it is.

TAUNTER #1: Holy shit!

TAUNTER #2: You're very photogenic, y'know?!

TAUNTER #3: Hey, thumbs up, bitch!

TAUNTER #4: What a hideous representation of your country you are, young lady!

TAUNTER #5: You fuckin' cretin!!!

TAUNTER #2: You should be in prison for life, you pieca' shit…!

TAUNTER #6: *(Over "…shit…")* How dare you!

TAUNTER #4: *(Over "…dare you…")* You're worse than the fuckin' terrorists!

TAUNTER #1: *(Over "…terrorists…")* You should do that child a favor and give it to someone who hasn't disgraced their country!

TAUNTER #3: *(Over "…country…")* You're a savage!

TAUNTER #5: (*Over "...savage..."*) If I wasn't a Liberal, I'd say they should string you up by your eyelids!

TAUNTER #6: (*Over "...eyelids..."*) If I wasn't a Conservative, I'd say they should string you up by your eyelids!

TAUNTER #4: (*Over "...eyelids..."*) How d'you sleep?!!!

TAUNTER #1: You're a disgrace!

TAUNTER #2: You're a disgrace!

TAUNTER #3: You're a disgrace!

TAUNTER #4: You're a disgrace!

TAUNTER #5: You're a disgrace!

ALL TAUNTERS: A DISGRACE!!!!!!

JENNY: GO AWAAAAAAAAAAAAAAAAAAAAAY!!!!!!!!!!

(This last line reverberates, like an echo, as JENNY protectively covers her baby. The Taunters fade, as if with the tide...)

(After a moment, a light change, as SHERRY escorts JENNY, emotionally worn, with baby.)

SHERRY: And last but not least, heeeeere's our livingroom.

JENNY: It's yours, Sherry.

SHERRY: Hey, enougha' that "yours" stuff. This is your place as much as it is mine, okay? You got a bedroom for yourself and little Patricia, and we split the bathroom, kitchen, the rest, just like we talked about, okay? It's not much, but...

JENNY: It's plenty, Sher. Believe me. You've done so much...

SHERRY: *(Over "so much...")* Nope, I don't wana' hear it. I'm still givin' the tour, okay? *(As if to keep spirits up, she looks out....)* And look, right outside that glass door is the patio viewin' the ocean. See that?

JENNY: *(A weak, indulging smile.)* It's...it's beautiful, Sher.

SHERRY: Far cry from Halibut, huh?

JENNY: Yeah, you ain't kiddin'...

SHERRY: Lemme tell ya', whenever you need to clear your head or just need time to de-stress, just go out there. Cheaper than a shrink, I'm tellin' ya'.

JENNY: Okay.

SHERRY: Now come on, take a load off. Shit, you've been on your feet enough since you been out, right?

JENNY: Thanks.

> *(They sit, and look at each other; SHERRY smiling enough for two, while JENNY is attempting to keep her best face on, though it is clear that she is having difficulty...)*

SHERRY: My God, I can't believe you're here.

JENNY: I know, right?

SHERRY: I'm so happy to have ya'.

JENNY: *(Pause.)* Sherry?

SHERRY: What's up, hon?

JENNY: Why…why are you…?

SHERRY: Stop it before you start, okay?

JENNY: Why would you…?

SHERRY: Jenny,…

JENNY: No, Sherry, I mean, people hate me.

SHERRY: *(Slight pause.)* That's 'cause they don't know you. They know what they wana' know.

JENNY: But they still…

SHERRY: Look, everything I put in my letters, I meant. If you want me to repeat everything, then you're gonna' make me soak my new blouse, okay? Now at some point they're gonna' jus' have to get over themselves and move on with their lives, just like you.

JENNY: Sherry, I don't want you to get hurt.

SHERRY: Jenny…

JENNY: No, Sherry, really, this could be…

SHERRY: *(Over "this could be…")* Hey, girl, let me worry about myself, okay? They can't hurt me anymore than I've been. You just worry about that beautiful little thing in your arms. Okay? *(Leans over to them…)* Look at that gorgeous creature. Eyes like her mommy.

JENNY: *(Weakly smiles, unable to look at baby.)* Hm.

SHERRY: You named her after your mom, right?

JENNY: Yeah.

SHERRY: C'mon, you're not even lookin' at 'er.

JENNY: I know what she looks like, Sher. I know. *(Slight pause, with great difficulty.)* Y'know,…you'd think it'd be easy to look into the eyes of the one thing that doesn't have a clue what the world thinks of ya',…but actually it's not. It's even harder.

SHERRY: *(Slight pause.)* Well,…I know she looks at you'n all she sees is the woman responsible for her life.

JENNY: Shit, n'look what kinda' life.

SHERRY: Honey, c'mon…

JENNY: I mean, Sher, she didn't ask for this. Y'know? There's landmines on the ground n'she ain't even learned to walk yet. I mean…

SHERRY: *(With a smile…)* Hey, you like ham?

JENNY: Uh…ye…sure.

SHERRY: No, not just ham, darlin'. Ham with freakin' Jersey tomatoes. Oh, you don't know, girl.

JENNY: *(A tepid snicker…)* Okay.

SHERRY: *(Slight pause.)* Everything's gonna' be okay.

JENNY: *(Slight pause, a weak smile.)* Okay.

SHERRY: Alright?

JENNY: Yeah.

SHERRY: *(Slight pause, smiling…)* Go ahead and put on the tube, if y'want. I'll go make us some lunch.

JENNY: Thanks, Sher.

SHERRY: Hey. No shit. *(A beat.)* I'm really glad you're here. Okay? Wouldn't have it any other way.

(They smile at each other, before SHERRY goes off.)

(JENNY takes a considerable moment to absorb this, before simulating turning on TV with remote.)

(We see the rest of the ensemble in dim light around her, who speak the following as if a singular news cast...)

NEWSCASTER 1: Just weeks after her release,...

NEWSCASTER 2: she has been sighted in our very own...

NEWSCASTER 3: Garden State, as shown in this amateur video shot...

NEWSCASTER 4: today of her waiting at a Central New Jersey bus stop. -

NEWSCASTER 5: Whether she actually plans to reside here is...

NEWSCASTER 6: currently unknown. However,...

NEWSCASTER 1: this would lead one to believe that...

NEWSCASTER 2: Miss Pitts, a...

NEWSCASTER 3: well-documented Texas native, is...

NEWSCASTER 4: attempting to avoid the spotlight...

NEWSCASTER 5: of infamy that has been on her since...

NEWSCASTER 6: the revelation of those horrific…

NEWSCASTER 1: photos -

NEWSCASTER 2: from -

NEWSCASTER 3: Baghdad.

ALL NEWSCASTERS: Whether she will ever truly overcome the stigma of her actions remains…

> *(She turns off television. Stares at it, with great pain for a considerable moment.)*
>
> *(She then suddenly rises, looks off where SHERRY has exited, uncertain and lost.)*
>
> *(Eventually, …she slowly walks to the area of the patio door and we soon hear the sounds of the ocean.)*
>
> *(She looks out for a considerable moment, as if the ocean is not doing what SHERRY had claimed, …before a soft cry from her baby prompts Jenny to look at her…for a long, emotional moment.)*
>
> *(Eventually, Jenny smiles, holds the baby close, and begins a soothing hum akin to a lullaby…)*
>
> *(The Lights eventually fade…as do the sounds of the distant waves…)*

End of Play

Daniel Damiano is an Award-winning Playwright, Actor, Screenwriter, Poet and Novelist based in Brooklyn, NY. His plays have been performed throughout many areas of the U.S., as well as London, England and Sydney & Melbourne, Australia. His acclaimed play DAY OF THE DOG premiered with St. Louis Actors' Studio in 2013 and subsequently transferred to 59E59 in NYC in 2014. It was a 2013 St. Louis Critics Choice Best Play Nominee, and is published by Broadway Play Publishing. His more recent play THE WILD BOAR was a 2022 Finalist for Dayton Playhouse's Futurefest, as well as a previous Finalist for both the 2019 Woodward/Newman Drama Award and the Janet & Bruce Bunch Award. He was the recipient of the Christopher Brian Wolk Award for his play DREAMS OF FRIENDLY ALIENS, which premiered with Abingdon Theatre Company. He was a 2013 Nominee for the Pushcart Poetry Prize and a Finalist for the 2012 Arts & Letters Prize for Drama. His debut novel, THE WOMAN IN THE SUN HAT *(Seattle Book Review Recommendation)* was published in March 2021 through fandango 4 Art House. His short story, *The Gift of What For* is included in Palm Circle Press' Short Story Anthology 2021. His poetry book, 104 DAYS OF THE PANDEMIC, was released in September 2021, by fandango 4 Art House. His poetry has been published in Crooked Teeth Literary Magazine, Newtown Literary Journal, New Voices Anthology, Cloudbank and HotMetal Press. His latest solo play, ONE WITH THE CURRENT, premiered in the 2022 Dream Up Festival at Theater for the New City in NYC. His forthcoming novel is GRAPHIC NATURE.

MESSAGE TO ACTORS & PRODUCERS:

Actors are welcome to use excerpts from these plays for the purposes of acting and scene-study classes as well as auditions, but it is *strongly* requested that the author's name and play title be clearly noted.

Theatre producers, if there is interest in any of these works for public performance, please reach out to the publisher of this collection, fandango 4 Art House, or to the Playwright directly, as noted in the introduction.

We at fandango 4 Art House also welcome all readers to share their reviews, most notably on its Goodreads and/or Amazon pages, and welcome recommendations to local bookstores.

Thank you.

***

Recently Published Works by Daniel Damiano

DAY OF THE DOG
(Broadway Play Publishing)

THE WOMAN IN THE SUN HAT (Novel)
(fandango 4 Art House)

104 DAYS OF THE PANDEMIC (Poetry)
(fandango 4 Art House)

THE GIFT OF WHAT FOR (Short Story)
Palm Circle Press Short Story Anthology 2021
(Palm Circle Press)